D1453152

TRUST YOUR OWN VOICE

GROWING YOUR INFLUENCE THROUGH CONFIDENT COMMUNICATION

KAREN LAOS

Kim –

thanks for your
business! Excited for
the April event.

Always remember that
your voice is powerful!

Karen

The stories in this book reflect the author's recollection of events. Some names, locations, and identifying characteristics have been changed to protect the privacy of those depicted. Dialogue has been re-created from memory.

ENDORSEMENTS

"Karen is gifted in her ability to convey important content in an accessible and personal way. Her warmth and information are a highly effective combination."

— DR. JOHN TOWNSEND, AUTHOR OF BOUNDARIES, LEADERSHIP COACH AND ORGANIZATIONAL CONSULTANT

"You made a lasting impression on this cohort. It was our highest rated session in two years! We have not stopped receiving positive feedback! Thank you for speaking at our women's leadership event."

— CLAIRE MAYERHOFER, UNITEDHEALTHCARE

"You received some of the highest scores I have ever seen for one of our "non governance" conference sessions."

— OPHELIA KING, VICE PRESIDENT OF EVENTS, SOCIETY FOR CORPORATE GOVERNANCE

"The time you spent in Boston, simply put, was outstanding. The information and knowledge will be put into practice immediately. As a point of fact – you are best in class; your energy and smile are contagious, and the fact that you modeled everything you were discussing really makes the case and point."

— KERRI BAILEY, MANAGER, MEDIA SALES, YAHOO!

"Thank you so much for today's training. I found it to be incredibly helpful and I know that our team did, as well. I've heard people reflecting on some of your pointers in their interactions with each other and that says it all."

— BONNI POMUSH, CEO, WORKING WARDROBES

"Since we've worked together, I've been asked to host a number of events both internally and externally, and I've been asked to create coaching curriculums for a few of the firms we work with. I owe you a lot of the credit because you helped me think strategically and helped me learn how to communicate more effectively. You've had an amazing impact on me! It was so much fun working with you, and I gained so much out of it. You've helped elevate my communication."

— JILL KNOLL, INVESTMENT MANAGEMENT PROFESSIONAL, LOS ANGELES

IF YOU WANT 9 WORDS TO AVOID
AND WHAT TO SAY INSTEAD, SCAN
THIS QR CODE:

To you, dear reader, as one of 10 million women who will overcome self-doubt and speak with confidence:

I celebrate you.

Your voice can change the world.

CONTENTS

FOREWORD

Conversation circa 2009 with Dr. John Townsend, Author of Boundaries, Leadership Coach and Organizational Consultant:

John: "You've got a book in you, Karen."

Me, shrugging it off: "Everybody thinks they've got a book in them. What makes you think *I* do?"

John: "Because the world needs hope. And, you give people hope."

INTRODUCTION

TRANSFORM YOUR LIFE

You're holding back.

You want to share your ideas, but you hesitate.

You doubt yourself.

You don't want to say the wrong thing.

You don't want to be judged.

You don't want to rock the boat.

What a debilitating way to live!

You want to speak up without hesitation.

You want to be free.

Many women are living with external confidence, but inside, they're full of self-doubt. I see this all the time with my clients who are high-achieving senior-level leaders.

We walk into a room and feel less than, even unworthy. We feel like an imposter.

I remember sitting in leadership meetings thinking, "I should speak up! I have a good idea!" But I'd stay silent because I didn't trust that I would say it right or that it would be seen as something of value. Then, the moment would pass.

Sound familiar?

If you've ever held back from sharing your ideas, you're not alone. There's an army of women who can relate. I've been there, too.

The best news of all? You can overcome it. You can get past holding yourself back and share your ideas freely.

You can know what to say and how to say it. When you do, your brain and emotions will be freed from the fear of not saying it right, being judged, and rocking the boat.

In this book, you'll learn how to show up differently; to show up as your true self with your true voice. You'll get sentence prompts and specific tools that you can practice right away.

You'll learn how to trust your own voice and empower yourself.

You'll be equipped to free yourself from worrying about what everyone is thinking about you. You can shift from the inside out. It's about feeling free to be yourself. With freedom comes confidence.

What are some tangible outcomes of confidence?

- "I now go to meetings and speak first."
- "My proposal was accepted [as is] in less than 24 hours after my presentation!"
- "I wasn't freaking out with anxiety because I felt confident."
- "I was able to set a boundary that I couldn't before!"

You'll learn how to build trust and credibility quickly through your voice. For example, you might be the best kept secret in your industry. If you can't communicate what you do and do it in a way that's likable, approachable, and connecting, then people aren't going to listen to you.

Reading this book will give you techniques to know exactly what to do to be a confident communicator and an influential leader.

COMMUNICATE WITH CONFIDENCE EVERY DAY

This is for everyday communication so you can grow your influence in any situation. This is not just for public speaking. In fact, when are we "private speaking" anyway? Unless you're talking to yourself in the shower or in the car, you always have an audience. This is a mindset shift. You have to think about these techniques from the perspective of anytime you open your mouth to speak.

Many people hire me for a high-stakes meeting or event. I love it when a woman hires me because she wants to speak with confidence in all areas of her life, and she recognizes the importance of how she would stand out as a result of that.

HOW TO READ THIS BOOK

If you're anything like me, you want to get past the fluff and get to the point. You're busy and overextended. I see you!

I designed this book with how I like to read: quickly and efficiently. Get me to the meat as soon as possible. You can pick up any chapter that interests you and in any order.

My recommendation? Read Chapter 1 first. It's the story that catapulted me to overcome my fear of holding back. My guess is that you'll relate to it. That's my transformation story.

FUN TO MEET YOU

Originally from the suburbs of Minneapolis, I've lived in San Francisco since 1994. I threw a bunch of clothes in the trunk of my car to follow a dream of living here, and once I arrived, I never left. I have an adventurous spirit and a huge heart for people.

Professionally, I've been fortunate to work with companies like NASA, Google, and Netflix. I left my corporate role in

2020 at 52 years of age to follow my entrepreneurial dream and fulfill my mission: to reach 10 million women to overcome self-doubt and speak with confidence. I've never looked back.

The thing that people say most about working with me is that they feel comfortable around me. I care deeply and make people feel safe. That's my relational side. My intention is to create a positive space where you feel seen, heard, and celebrated for exactly who you are. I have a zest for life and always see the positive side of things.

On the tactical side, people get results from working with me. You'll feel more confident quickly. You'll get practical tips with a how-to formula that you can immediately apply.

I continue to hear again and again: "Wow, I can use this right now!"

As one client said, "You speak the truth in love." People know that they're not going to get fluff or lip service with me. I'm going to tell you how it is, but I'll tell you in an encouraging way and show you how to change.

My favorite compliment that I get often is "You're in my head!" around what to say and how to say it. A whole group of clients got together and gave me a mug that said, "What would Karen say?" That's the ultimate praise!

NO PERMISSION NEEDED

Let's burst out of the box we put ourselves in and step into our confidence. No permission needed. Take your seat at the table and be the unstoppable force you were meant to be.

Each woman reading this book needs to look inward and recognize this important and inarguable fact: You are a masterpiece. Live in the freedom of being unapologetically you.

Trust your own voice and I'll guide you to becoming a confident communicator one step at a time.

I'm here for you!

Love,
Karen

YOU CAN EMPOWER YOURSELF

Everyone was staring at me. Sitting in the boardroom attempting to present, I was tongue-tied. Looking down at my notes, my halted speech continued. Six leadership team peers—including Sue, the company president—were gently suggesting ways to proceed while I struggled to express myself. I felt so stupid.

The problem? I didn't agree with what I was supposed to present. It didn't make sense. My boss, Sue, had suggested months prior that I lead this discussion. It didn't make sense then, and it didn't make sense now, but I never said anything. I chose to go with it even though I disagreed. I figured she knew better.

Trapped by my internal conflict of what I was taught ("Don't question your boss because she knows best and you need to respect her authority") versus my own knowing that this idea didn't make sense, I stumbled over my words. After several awkward moments, Sue swooped in and kindly suggested we table the discussion. I was grateful yet mortified.

Afterward, she pulled me into her office. "Today was a perfect example of you not trusting your gut, Karen. You could've stopped and said, 'I don't even remember why we were doing this in the first place. Let's table it.'"

Seriously? That would've never occurred to me. Could it really be that easy? I thought I *had* to do what my boss said, regardless of whether I agreed. I was so embarrassed.

"Why do I still need permission to speak up?" I thought. "I'm in my 40s, for goodness sake! And I'm a senior leader with decades of experience. Why can't I trust myself?."

Can you relate?

All I wanted was to share my ideas without hesitation.

To stop holding back and confidently speak up—even if my ideas were unpopular.

To act without needing other people's permission.

To overcome the fear of what other people would think.

To stop doubting myself and trust my gut.

To trust my own voice.

To be free.

What about you? You may have felt this way with a teacher, parent, or sibling, struggling to voice your ideas, your opinions—struggling to find your voice. I've coached thousands of women, and it's an issue, even among senior leaders. It's sobering to realize how many of us have had similar experiences.

Most of the problem stems from our past.

VOICES THAT FORM US

Growing up, my dad never really saw me. He never said, "I love you" or "I'm proud of you." He beamed to his buddies on the tennis court about my accomplishments, but never to me. Once he dropped me off at the Minneapolis airport as a young adult, and I decided to say "I love you" to see what he would do. His eyes awkwardly met mine and then quickly moved to the car floor.

He was emotionally detached and a man of few words. One entire summer, he ignored me for not putting "enough" gas in the car.

He would take me on walks to downtown Minneapolis, but talked *at* me the whole time, lecturing about things that didn't interest me, such as the history of the train tracks. He didn't enter *my* world. He never heard me. My voice didn't seem to matter. I desperately wanted a connection with him, but my attempts to get his approval were futile and left me feeling worthless.

When I was thirteen, I poured out my heart to him in a letter, hoping to reach him so things could be better between us.

He never opened it.

For two weeks, my mom would make the bed and put it back on his pillow.

Two weeks straight.

He never opened it.

---

*I WONDERED IF MY VOICE WAS IMPORTANT—
OR IF I MATTERED.*

I felt invisible.

After two weeks, it was Mom who ended up opening my letter. Inside, she found her daughter's heart on the pages, desperately attempting to reach her father. But she said nothing to him about it because you didn't question my father.

Even though I was never explicitly told I didn't have a voice, that's what was modeled to me. In my house, I learned that it's better to stay silent in order to keep the peace.

I wanted her to stand up for me—to stand up for herself. But she didn't.

Mom was a nurturing homemaker raising nine kids who submitted to my dad's authority. I was taught to believe that the authority figure knows best, and therefore, my voice as a woman wasn't important enough to be heard.

Only two times in my childhood can I recall her crying. When I was ten years old, she was changing the sheets and shared with me that Dad wouldn't let her take a job as a secretary at St. Peter's Church. All she wanted was a little independence and a purpose of her own outside the home, but she wasn't given permission. The second time was when I was 12. I found her upstairs, hunched over her sewing machine, in tears. Dad wouldn't let her travel to my brother's last football game as the quarterback at Dartmouth. She had never been to one game.

Mom often diminished her value. Whenever she would phone someone, her opening words were, "Sorry to bother you."

These moments confused me. I felt frustrated, angry, and helpless. She was an adult, a peer of my dad. Why wouldn't she do what she wanted? He had ignored her for days in the past when she went against his will. She said she couldn't take the silence.

Yet, Mom was a powerhouse leader in the community. She led ministries at church and a branch of the local Little League. She was publicly recognized as an influential leader—there, she used her voice. She led people and meetings. I witnessed this when she brought my siblings and me to events. I saw her use her voice confidently in those settings. It was conflicting to watch her at home when Mom chose to set aside her needs and her voice to accommodate my dad's. I learned from her that everyone else—and everyone else's voices—came first.

MIXED MESSAGES

Mom and Dad sent me conflicting messages with their actions and their choices. Mom spoke up outside the home but restrained her voice around Dad. Did this mean a woman's voice should be squelched around men and authority figures (who were usually one and the same)? Yet, she did speak up in the community, often in meetings that included men. What was I supposed to learn? Was it okay to speak up, or was it better to fall silent and let others speak?

These mixed messages from Dad were complex: on one hand I was suppressed—he didn't even bother to open the letter, to read what I had to say! On the other hand, I was empowered—he taught me to speak up for myself. He taught me the power of asking and often said, "The squeaky wheel gets the grease."

Have you received any mixed messages from authority figures in your life?

I HAD TO EMPOWER MYSELF

My dad wouldn't listen to my deepest pain, my deepest desires, even when I carefully worded them in a letter. I wanted to be heard and I tried creative ways to do so, but nothing worked. He didn't seem to care what I had to say.

Mom couldn't find or trust her own voice around my dad, so I lacked a strong female role model to show me how to speak with confidence.

If only they would've reassured me that my voice mattered.

What I needed was to feel safe and accepted without criticism, knowing I wouldn't be judged if I shared something unpopular or that rocked the boat.

My parents couldn't give me that safety or acceptance. I've come to realize no one could do that for me.

WHAT *I* NEEDED WAS TO EMPOWER MYSELF.

THE CHALLENGE

I had to become someone who isn't dependent upon others to give me permission to speak. I had to believe that my ideas mattered. That I mattered. That I had valuable things to say even if someone disagreed with me. I had to get to the point where I didn't need anyone's approval.

But how? It felt like an impossible task.

The summer before entering high school, I turned the tables on my dad. For eight years prior, I attended St. Peter's, the Catholic school in my hometown of Richfield, Minnesota. For my freshman year, I wanted to go to the public school, Richfield High. My dad wanted me to go to

Holy Angels, the Catholic high school, so that was the plan. There was no debate or discussion with him. You did what he said. It was hard to interact with him, to be heard. In an early attempt to empower myself, I tried to convince him otherwise. He still said "no."

A WAY TO REACH HIM

My plan was to get cut from the tennis team. That was the only way I had a chance. Dad was proud of my tennis game. He had worked hard to make me as good as I was. Ever since I was six, he made me play every day, and at first, I hated it because it was a "have to."

I ended up being grateful that he made me play, as I enjoyed being confident on the court.

Fast forward to the day he got the call from the Holy Angels tennis coach. Befuddled, he couldn't believe I was cut. He didn't know I swallowed my pride all summer and lobbed those balls as far out of the court as possible. I had a mission. And I accomplished it. I didn't know what would come of it; I only knew that was my best course of control. Two days before Richfield started, Dad said, "Do you want to go to Richfield?" I said, "*Yes!*" and he mumbled, "Well, you can go," and walked out of my room.

Victory! It worked. I went on to be a star on the tennis team, and he came to almost every game.

DAD'S GREATEST GIFTS

Despite my dad's emotional distance, he built into me two of my greatest gifts: the belief that I can do anything and the boldness to take action.

For example, he often assembled the entire neighborhood to advocate for causes he believed in. He wouldn't hesitate to knock on doors for signatures. He was relentless. He may not have entered my world, but I was watching his world. He made things happen.

Dad first taught me how to negotiate at a flea market when I was six years old. He put a few dollars in my hand to go shopping and told me never to take full price.

I had no problem asking. I felt empowered using my voice. I found it quite exhilarating. It was a thrill to see if I could woo the person to give me a lower price.

By the time I was a young adult, I had experimented with different techniques to be heard. Lassoing the good gift from my dad—to be bold enough to take action—I started speaking up in my new role as a Mary Kay consultant.

FAKE IT TIL YOU MAKE IT

At 18 years old, I made a killing. Trained by my dad to be fearless, I would go up to anyone and ask for her opinion. I was booking facials and making sales. This is where I learned the concept "Fake it Til You Make it." Every Monday night, I would attend the Mary Kay sales meetings, where they taught us that you'd never know every detail of the product, but you'll want to act as you do.

With this training, I gained confidence and overcame some of the conflicting messages from my parents. I had a natural warmth that drew people to me. Ever since I was a kid, people have felt comfortable around me. I leveraged that without realizing it by simply being myself, and it worked.

ACT AS IF

Simultaneously, I was taking ballroom dance classes at Arthur Murray. I'll never forget when I walked into the studio, and another student asked me if I was an instructor. *"Who, me? What?"*

He smiled. *"You walked in so confidently, I thought you were in charge!"*

What an impact on my 18-year-old self! From that point on, I walked into rooms with my shoulders back and head held high.

How is this the same young woman who held back due to fear of what other people would think—to the point where I missed out on opportunities because I didn't fully express my true self?

I can't be sure it was my confident stride and bold moxie that led to my success, but I was a leader in high school:

class president and co-captain of the tennis team, and I traveled for national marketing competitions through an organization called DECA: Distributive Education Clubs of America. These opportunities counteracted the confusion of home, helping me see that I did have a voice and that I could be heard.

Years later, in business, I'm the one who always asks. I've created my own job three times in my career—making a case for myself and advocating for why I'm the best person for the role. I'm a fearless negotiator (thanks, Dad!).

In retrospect, I see the tools piling up that formed me:

- Believe you can do anything
- Be bold enough to take action
- Fake it Til You Make It
- Be yourself
- Leverage your natural strengths to influence others
- Stand tall and walk with confidence
- Always negotiate

Even a car dealership owner told me that I wore him out. That wasn't my intention, but I was committed to getting the best deal. I'm relentless, as my dad was.

A few years into my job as a corporate trainer, my boss said she wanted to hear more from me in meetings—that my voice is valuable. "When you speak up," she said, "you have great input."

I walked out of her office feeling excited and also conflicted. Part of me—the flea-market negotiator, the class president, the Mary Kay sales rep—stood taller, prouder. Another part—the girl whose father never opened her letter, never valued her voice—felt hesitant, unsure.

My boss had many of my dad's characteristics and equally conflicting messages. Sometimes when I or others spoke up, she dismissed those ideas. Did she really mean it when she said I should speak up? Why speak up if she might veto it anyway?

I remained confident with clients and my direct reports, but I found myself holding back when it came to our leadership team, of which I was a part. Even though I knew my perspective was valued, I kept quiet much of the time. I didn't feel safe. I came across as wishy-washy. I would go with the majority or what I thought my boss wanted to hear. I'm not proud of that. I wish I had believed in myself enough to share my ideas more often.

With each meeting, I felt trapped, conflicted, and hesitant to share what I really thought. Sometimes, I would be close to saying something, but then the moment would pass. It grated on me. I wanted to overcome it!

YOU CAN EMPOWER YOURSELF

Sue was both my biggest challenger and my strongest champion. Her personality held me back, but her encouragement to trust my gut made me aware that I had a pattern of not doing that. I had to get to the root of the problem. I knew I needed to examine my past in order to empower myself.

YOU CAN LEARN TO TRUST YOUR OWN VOICE AND EMPOWER YOURSELF, TOO.

There is hope, and that's why I'm writing this book. For *you*. You can overcome the self-doubt messages from your past and speak with confidence. You can stop holding back and be free.

THE PATH TO GROWTH STARTS WITH HEALING

My healing journey with Dr. John Townsend and Dennis Del Valle over ten years in the Townsend Leadership Program taught me how to get my emotional needs met. I didn't even know I had needs until I was 40 years old. I grew up with a mom who ignored her emotional needs. That's the model I followed. You live for everyone else: make them happy whatever the cost.

I learned about boundaries, recognizing that "no" is a complete sentence (tips for you in Chapter 8).

I learned the power of grieving. The process sucks, but the healing is worth it. This included saying goodbye to my dad and grieving other losses from my past.

Therapy helped. As I began to learn the power of feeling my feelings, my therapist told me to put my hand on the spot where I was feeling the emotion physically. It was in my stomach. When I put my hand there, I couldn't help but think, "I'm paying you $150 an hour to feel my stomach?! Let's get to the point!" I've come to realize that *is* the point. When we learn how to feel and lean into the feeling, it eventually will pass. It will not overwhelm us. It's the path to healing.

I learned to ask for what I needed. I felt empowered with the comfort and strength of being known.

AFTER YEARS OF THIS DEDICATION TO GROWTH, I FINALLY GOT TO THE POINT WHERE I ACTUALLY BELIEVED THAT I MATTERED—AND SO DID MY IDEAS.

You can heal from whatever is holding you back. When you get the right support, you're on your way to growth. It will take time, but it's possible. You're on your way to empowering yourself. Empowered people speak up for themselves. That's what I want for you.

MY TRANSFORMATION MOMENT

One of the first times I pushed back with Sue during a meeting was months after my tongue-tied moment in the boardroom. I proposed an idea, and she waved her hand with a dismissive gesture. I almost shut up, but then I thought, "No, my idea is important." So I pushed back again. She ultimately disagreed, but I'm proud that I spoke up. It felt good to stand up for myself.

Even when your ideas don't get used, there's still value in speaking up and owning your opinions. The fact that someone dismisses them doesn't diminish them. This is why a lot of women stop speaking up: because we put too much value on what the other person thinks.

WE NEED TO REALIZE THAT EVEN WHEN SOMEONE DISAGREES, YOUR IDEAS—AND YOU —ARE STILL WORTHY.

That never changes.

In a conversation with Sue, I asked what she thought about an issue. She quipped, "I don't know, Karen, what do *you* think? You always ask others first. I want to know what *you* think." My jaw dropped. I never recognized this pattern. Upon reflection, I realized I would typically come to a meeting asking everyone else what they thought and rarely spoke up. Or, I would wait and go along with the most popular vote.

This pattern had to stop. I realized I could no longer keep myself trapped. It was time to free myself.

Back in the boardroom, during another leadership meeting, I had my moment.

FOR THE FIRST TIME, INSTEAD OF WAITING, I SPOKE FIRST: "HERE'S MY VOTE."

I shared my opinion in a way that felt right for me. I was no longer hiding, and it was exhilarating!

No one died or rejected me. Sue didn't wave her hand dismissively, but even if she did, I knew I would never go back. I would venture to say that I was even more respected. More importantly, I trusted my own voice—no matter the consequences of speaking up.

EQUIPPING WOMEN TO SPEAK UP

It's been a transformative journey. Finding my voice is the most empowering thing I've done for myself. My story has become my calling.

In fact, for the past several years, I've been teaching women how to trust their own voices. My profession is in communication. I'm a keynote speaker and stand on stages equipping women with the tools needed to overcome self-doubt and speak with confidence. I love supporting women with how to build trust and credibility quickly through their voice, presence, and message.

My mission is to reach 10 million women—women like you, like me. Anyone who has ever sat in a boardroom or classroom or laundry room and felt silenced. Imagine if we all felt free to speak up in a way that honored ourselves and brought the best version of us to light!

CONSIDER THIS YOUR INVITATION. IF YOU DON'T TRUST YOUR OWN VOICE, TODAY CAN BE YOUR MOMENT.

You can overcome the self-doubt from your past that causes you to hold back.

You can be confident in your own voice.

You can speak up without hesitation.

You can empower yourself.

You can be free.

2

OVERCOME SELF-DOUBT

Sometimes even seeing the phrase "overcome self-doubt" seems unfathomable. Can you actually "overcome" it? Most of us doubt ourselves at some point, and it's hard to remove it completely, but we can definitely lessen it such that it loses power over us.

For most of my life I had this internal conflict related to speaking up. But, when it came to me sharing something I knew was of value to others, I had no problem speaking up.

I did well professionally because I was confident. I believed that I could do anything.

When selling Mary Kay, people were drawn to me and drawn to the product because not only did I believe in it, I believed in them and sincerely wanted to give them more confidence. At that time, it was in their appearance, but it was almost magical. I could help them feel beautiful, hopeful, happy, and confident. All from a little make-up! I like to think it had something to do with my belief in them, too.

ACT AS IF

If you act "as if" you're confident, your mind and body follow. The cool thing, too, is that our subconscious mind doesn't know the difference between what's real and what's not, so acting the part is half the battle. That's the stepping stone to actually becoming confident—that along with action. We have to step into it.

For example, when working for Mary Kay, I thought of everyone as a potential customer. Servers at restaurants, people shopping next to me at Macy's, you name it. I would make a genuine connection with them (that's key!) and then invite them over to my parent's house and give them a facial! It worked.

MISSED OPPORTUNITIES

A story that is seared in my brain (and body!) is this: I was 22 and on stage for rehearsal in Tucson, Arizona, sitting around with 100 other cast members on the risers listening to our director give instructions. I had accepted that I didn't get the lead singing or dancing parts.

As he ran through rehearsal notes, he suddenly realized that he had a speaking part unassigned, and he called out: "Who wants to do this speaking part?" Everything in me wanted to raise my hand, but I hesitated.

Within seconds, the girl next to me raised her hand, and he handed her the piece of paper to read from, and she got the part. Just like that! I was so disappointed. Huge lesson learned. It was a big price to pay.

ALL YEAR SHE HAD THAT PART, AND I USED TO WATCH HER ON STAGE OCCASIONALLY AND THINK, "THAT COULD'VE BEEN ME."

All because of self-doubt.

So what do we do about it? How do we get rid of it?

I've got a few exercises to help you:

AFFIRMATIONS

One of my all-time favorite exercises to call in what you want to feel or be is affirmations. I've always been a big believer in personal growth, so it was an easy sell, but I still have to tell you I only "trusted the system." I wasn't 100% positive that they worked.

Here's when I became convinced: a few years ago, I decided that I wanted to represent radiance in the world and be more of a light to others. I chose the affirmation "I am radiant" and started saying it all the time to myself, as well as putting Post-its up on my mirror and around the house saying the same thing.

Within a short timeframe, I had *two* people tell me I was radiant. What?! One was in written feedback after a corporate training program I had facilitated.

I was stunned. Who uses the word "radiant" anyway? Especially in a corporate setting. I was convinced that affirmations work.

Here's the key: pick a short phrase (I recommend one at a time) and repeat it several times a day. Write it on Post-its and place them all over your house: bathroom mirror, nightstand; wherever you're going to see the affirmation regularly. It will help you lean into what it is that you want to be.

Sample affirmations could be:

I am unstoppable
People love to hear what I have to say
I speak with confidence and clarity
I'm an incredible mom
I speak with power
I'm amazing at my job
I bring great value to the world
I'm lovable

There's some research out there suggesting our subconscious best solidifies things either right before we're going to bed or right as we're waking up. If you recite the affirmations several times, it may help. In my experience, saying them a few times a day has been enough.

The whole idea is that this is an experiment to try on - give it a go and see what you discover.

Naming your fears diminishes their power.

FEAR SCRIPT

This one is exactly how it sounds—a script between you and fear; a dialogue. Start by writing down the two roles:

1. Fear (played by my fear)

2. Me (played by you)

It might seem blatantly obvious what the roles are, but I explicitly state them both because sometimes we think they are one and the same. My goal is for you to see that they don't have to be. Fear is simply the old phrase "False Evidence Appearing Real."

NAME YOUR FEAR SO THAT YOU BECOME SEPARATE FROM IT.

If you see it that way, you'll be more successful in this exercise. Often, we internalize fear, and obviously, it is inside of us, but from a mindset perspective, acting as if it's outside of us can be really helpful so that it doesn't overpower or overtake us.

Here's how to do it. Start by writing "Fear" and then write down what fear is saying to you. Perhaps "I'm scared to share my real opinion because I'm afraid people won't like me," or "I'm scared to go for that job because I don't think I'm qualified." or "I'm afraid to leave my job to start my own business because it might not work out."

What does fear usually say to you? Insert your fear phrase here: _____.

The next step is to respond to fear as yourself. Let's take the first example.

Fear: "I'm afraid to leave my job to start my own business because it might not work out."

Me (or, in this case, you!): I can understand that. It can feel scary for sure. Do you know what's fascinating to think? What if it DOES work out?! We're so inclined to think things won't work out, and yet—imagine if you envisioned it the other way around—such a different perspective.

Fear: Wow, I hadn't thought of it that way. I'm still terrified that I won't be able to make enough money to pay my bills. And my benefits. That's scary!

Me: I can see why that feels scary. Here's a thought: what if you actually make more money than expected. Remember that time we got laid off? We made it. There's really no job security anyway. When a company needs to make ends meet and they can't keep you, they aren't thinking about you—they're taking care of themselves. You may want to think more about how betting on yourself may actually be the better security.

You can go back and forth as much as you like. Experiment with the dialogue and see what comes as a result. One of the objectives is to get more insights and clarity. The main goal would be that you start noticing, "Wow, I have all these messages of fear, but that's not actually me. I have responses back to fear that are very empowering," realizing that fear truly is just in your mind; technically something that you made up.

FACT VS. FEELING

Sometimes you're in a sticky situation; perhaps a conflict with someone, or you need to give difficult feedback to a person. This is an exercise to help you get clarity and avoid confusion.

On a piece of paper, make two columns with a heading for each: "Facts" and "Interpretations".

List the facts of the situation. As if you had recorded it on video—what would be the observable scene that no one could argue?

Then, list the various possible interpretations of that situation. I've done this when facilitating conflict with corporate teams.

Notice that the fact column is usually much shorter than the interpretations column, which includes our feelings and assumptions. It's fascinating! People can interpret it in so many different ways! It never ceases to amaze me. You can also list out the feelings people may be having with those interpretations.

Once you do that, notice what you discover, and you'll have more insights about the situation to inform you on what action to take.

R.A.I.N. (TARA BROCK'S MODEL)

This one is widely used in regards to fear. RAIN is an acronym representing the following:

- Recognize what is happening (roots of understanding)
- Allow life to be just as it is (grounds of love)
- Investigate with gentle attention (deepens understanding)
- Nurture (awakens love)

Experiment with it and see how it calms you.

GRIEVE

This is a big one. It wasn't until I was 40 through the Townsend Leadership Program that I realized grief expanded beyond the death of a loved one. It's about loss. Any loss that causes emotional strain of some sort.

I was raised in a Midwest household where what was culturally supported was "chin up" and move on—smile and swallow.

Stay positive and move forward regardless of the circumstances.

We didn't talk about emotions, let alone give space for loss. Consider a loss inventory—make a list of everything you've lost. It can be as big as the loss of a dream or as small as the loss of your Starbucks order being wrong when you're crunched for time. Set a timer for 20 minutes and jot down anything that comes to mind.

FORGIVE

Easier said than done: remember, forgiveness is for your freedom, not necessarily the other person—unless you're forgiving yourself! First, take the time to recognize who you need to forgive.

How did they wrong you, and what do you need to do to release that? Anything taking up space in your brain is sucking away at your energy and ability to feel free and fulfilled. Some call it mental load. It's all the things you're thinking about and feeling.

Another idea is to write a letter that you never send. Get all of your feelings out on paper and see how you feel. Sometimes getting it out is all you need. You could also role play with someone else. I find role plays extremely effective.

THE BROADWAY MUSICAL (MY PERSONAL FAVORITE):

This originates from a brilliant friend of mine, Rachel Grant, a neuroscience expert, sexual abuse recovery coach, and founder of the Beyond Surviving method for healing trauma.

She led this exercise at one of her workshops: sitting in a circle, 14 of us shared our strongest message of self-doubt. Messages like, "Who am I to be going for this promotion?" or "I'll never be good enough to start my own business," or "I don't deserve..."

After everyone shared, she sighed and said, "Feel the heaviness in the room?!" *Yes.* What a downer! Ha. She then said, "Now we're going to go around the room and say that same message, but sing it like a Broadway Musical, or at least say it in a totally different voice." Once we did that, we were all laughing hysterically. The room immediately became lighter.

SUDDENLY THAT MESSAGE OF DOUBT CARRIED SO MUCH LESS WEIGHT AND EVEN SEEMED KIND OF RIDICULOUS.

From a neuroscience perspective, this technique changes up your neural pathways so the meaning of the message shifts. It tricks your brain. Let's face it, singing "I'll never be good enough" at the top of your lungs has a way of showing you how silly that sounds.

NAME YOUR INNER CRITIC

This one is fun. Do you know the negative voice in your head? The one who says all those awful, discouraging, and judgemental things? If your inner critic had a name, what would that be?

The logic (like the Fear Script) is to name it—that act of naming takes the power away—the hold it has on you.

My inner critic's name is Gertrude. She's tall, skinny, with long gray hair that's pulled up really tight in a bun with wire-framed cat-eye glasses that sit halfway down her nose. She's always holding a clipboard with a pen judging me. The idea is to have it feel like it's outside of yourself. Then I could say, "Oh, Gertrude, just relax. It's going to be fine, it doesn't have to be perfect." That also gives the critical voice feeling some levity.

CHANGE YOUR FEAR NARRATIVE.

Another exercise is to tally the self-doubt or negative messages you say to yourself over a period of time, such as two days. Awareness is key. Notice how often you say these things in an average day. That's the first step. The second step is to find a positive message that resonates with you and prepare it as a counter-message every time you hear yourself saying that message of doubt.

The key to this is having it at the ready because if you don't, you're probably going to get sucked into that message of self-doubt. You've got to be ready to counteract that statement. Notice how things start to shift over time.

Bonus: Change your fear narrative. How could you begin shifting this?

Tip: when fear messages creep in have an opposite message ready to speak back to it.

My opposite message is_____.

Lastly, one of my dear friends who went through a divorce, heartbroken and full of doubt, said this: "Every day I would look at myself in the mirror and say 'You are beautiful.' At first, I felt weird doing it, but over time it got easier, and I even believed it! It works."

What is your biggest message of doubt?

What plagues you on a regular basis?

In my work now with thousands of women, the biggest themes are:

- Imposter syndrome (you think you don't belong or deserve a seat at the table)
- Fear of judgment
- Fear of rejection
- Fear of rocking the boat
- Fear of not being accepted
- People won't like you
- Perfectionism

So many themes, so little time!

THE KEY IS TO HIT YOUR SELF-DOUBT HEAD ON.

And know that you're not alone. We all have it. The question is, how much power does it hold over you? Commit to staying in control of it, so it doesn't control you.

Back to Arthur Murray. I was taken by the student saying that I walked in with so much confidence because that's the last thing I thought about myself at that time. This was a memorable moment for me. I was demonstrating confidence, and I didn't even realize it.

"Act as if" is the same idea. It's putting ourselves in the shoes of who or where we want to be. If we don't act the part that we want to be, or we don't act like the person that we want to show up as, it's going to be harder to get there.

If we think about ourselves as this is, for example: what would a writer do on a given day, what would a writer eat for breakfast, or what would a writer do in the afternoon, or what would a professional speaker do? Getting more connected to the vision that you're stepping into as if it's already happening with all of your emotions will move it closer to actually happening.

One of my favorite phrases is, "how would the person I want to be, do the thing I'm about to do?" This has been a guiding principle for me.

There's a real power behind the idea that you're acting as if it's already happened, so it's a lot easier for your subconscious brain to make it come to pass.

That's why vision boards are so powerful. We're putting out into the world what we want. Another exercise I love that has worked for me personally and for my clients is to journal as if your vision has already happened. For example, pick a future date that you want your dream to happen. Let's go with a year. Let's imagine it's June 29, 2022. On top of the page, you'd put June 29, 2023. Pretend it's that date and write as if it's already happened. Put as much emotion and anything related to the senses as possible. When we get our emotions involved, and we can feel it, touch it, smell it, taste it, and hear it—that's when things accelerate. It's amazing how many things on my vision board, as well as in my vision journaling practice, have come true.

FEAR OF JUDGMENT

Do you fear being judged?

I grew up with a perfectionist mom, and that rubbed off on me. She was kind and loving, so she didn't come across as critical, but I can still remember this: In the second grade of Catholic school, we had this assignment to make posters that were going to be up in the church for our first communion celebration. It was a poster made of felt (if you remember those!), and essentially *she* made it for me. She mapped it all out while I watched.

It looked amazing. It was the best looking poster in that church, but it was something she did. I was very proud of it, but it wasn't my work.

Mom also typed all of our papers in high school. *All* of them. If she had typed an entire page and made a mistake on the last line, she would throw the entire page out and type it over again. Thankfully, white-out was discovered by the time I was in high school!

One time as a college kid, I was watching her make the bed —she kept spreading her hands over the top of the bed, getting all of the wrinkles out. I remember saying, "Mom, it doesn't have to be perfect," to which she immediately retorted, "Honey, if you don't strive for perfection, you'll always be mediocre." Boom. There it is. The issue with that message is that anything other than perfect is unacceptable.

THIS NEED TO BE PERFECT IS PARALYZING.

It's directly connected to the fear of judgment.

RELEASING JUDGMENT

Fast forward to 2021: In Mountain View, CA, at a corporate training gig co-facilitating new material for the first time with the Chief Strategy Officer of the company. He was so supportive. He kept saying, do your thing. I'm conditioned (from my 20 years of corporate training experience) that there's a right way to do training modules, and you are judged on that.

In the two days that we worked together, I never felt like he was in the back with his clipboard judging me. My whole life, I have worked hard to overcome the doubt about not being perfect. I was always asking, "Am I going to measure up?" He gave me the most unusual and unexpected experience that turned my past on its head: He demonstrated that he respected and honored my expertise. Even though it was new material, he trusted me to do it.

He kept saying, "All that really matters, Karen, is the outcome. It doesn't matter that you use all the slides or the script. In fact, I'd prefer you ditch the script and focus on the outcome. What do we want the client to walk away with as a result of you delivering this module?" That was a milestone for me. It reminded me of the power of people being free to be themselves.

If you create an environment where this is encouraged, they'll be a lot more motivated and confident because they won't be worried about being judged.

RECORD YOURSELF

One of the best ways to get past self-doubt is to know how you're coming across.

I record and playback video with my clients regularly. It's what no one loves at first but quickly want more of because they see the value. It's the best way to see reality.

If you can't record yourself visually, then use audio. Record yourself at your next meeting. The more you can experience yourself in a real-life environment, the more effective it's going to be.

Here's how to do the playback: start by looking at the things you do well and then, secondly, the things that you could improve.

I always recommend that people watch their video objectively, almost as if it's someone else, because we're usually our own worst critics.

ASK, "WHAT DID THIS PERSON DO WELL?"

Then, after you give yourself a couple of positives that you're doing well, ask, what are a couple of things that you could work on?

I always start with the behavioral component: your style (see Chapters 3 and 4 for what to look for). Start there first because it doesn't matter how good your content is if you're not saying it in a way that's interesting. People aren't going to hear it anyway.

Your homework, if you choose to do it: pick ONE of these exercises to do this week. Let me know how it goes!

Let's banish self-doubt.

3

YOUR VOICE IS YOUR POWER

Your voice is powerful. And beautiful. The key is to know how to use it and ensure that you're representing yourself the way you want to be seen in the world.

For almost 20 years, I've been training people on how to influence through voice, presence, and messaging. Of all the components of leadership presence, voice is my favorite. It is the most nuanced and the most powerful. It has the most variety, which also means we can have the most fun with it (and the most impact).

EVERY TIME WE OPEN OUR MOUTHS, WE HAVE THE OPPORTUNITY TO INFLUENCE.

Many of my clients don't like the sound of their voices. Can you relate? As soon as they hear "record," they cringe. Yet, that's where the value lies. We have to be willing to see and hear ourselves the way others experience us. We need that objective reality. That starting point is gold because then we can know how to move forward.

BLIND SPOTS: ARE YOU MISREPRESENTING YOURSELF?

On January 9, 2021, I joined Clubhouse (the social media chat room app), and my world shifted. It became extremely obvious that our voices influence quickly. I know that people decide within seconds if they think you're credible, trustworthy, and likable, but wow, this app made that abundantly clear. There's a button called "Leave Quietly" which allows you to leave the virtual room. I used it a fair amount!

Here's what was sobering: the number of women misrepresenting themselves. It was mind boggling and reminded me that there is much work to be done.

For example, I have a friend with 25 years of experience in her field, and she was hosting a room for the first time (leading and moderating discussion). Marlene is a strong, well-spoken woman; a leader in her field.

She started that room so tentatively in her speech, and I thought, "Oh my gosh, this doesn't even sound like her." She came across as timid and meek; halting her voice with lots of awkward pauses. She wasn't taking charge or leading us in the conversation.

THAT WAS A REMINDER OF HOW MANY WOMEN ARE WALKING AROUND MISREPRESENTING THEMSELVES.

I was shocked at how different she sounded compared to how I know her.

I recognize that when faced with new environments, we may need a moment to adjust, but sadly, people are unforgiving when it comes to first impressions. The key is to be prepared and do whatever it takes to show up as our most confident selves.

I don't want you or anyone else to miss opportunities because of your voice. People decide so quickly, within nanoseconds, if they want to keep listening.

Are you coming across in a way that projects connection, as well as credibility? We've got to do both. Voice is a massive part of how people decide if you're worth listening to.

We don't naturally think about leveraging the strength in our voice, so it has to be intentional.

VOICE MECHANICS: VOLUME

Projection is one of the biggest opportunities for women. Simply put, speak louder.

Let's start with breathing. That's how we get our vocal power. Our entire body is part of how our voice sounds. We need that support. And when we're nervous, we tend to hold our breath, and then we lack the support needed to project with confidence.

Speak from the diaphragm, which is that wonderful muscle right below our stomach. It allows you to not only project using the proper support from your breath and, therefore, your entire body, but it also creates a richer tone compared to your voice coming from your throat.

I was coaching a woman who had a soft voice with no awareness of how timid she sounded. After we did a round of recording and listened back, she was surprised to hear how soft it truly was. In the second round, she spoke louder, but this time it was strained. It was coming from her throat.

When coaching women on projection, I notice the default is to raise our voices by using our throats to speak louder. Most of us are not conditioned to use our diaphragm.

I use the analogy of people going to a concert. You might be yelling or "happy screaming" for the person you love on stage. That kind of projection is not the voice we want to have when we're speaking in a meeting or in a negotiation.

We want to have that full support from the diaphragm so that the breath comes from there. If we don't, not only will we sound weaker, we'll kill our vocal cords over time.

Here's what to do about it:

EXERCISES FOR VOCAL PROJECTION

Think about it as if you're blowing up a balloon. Imagine your stomach being the balloon. See the air come in through your nose and down your throat and expand that balloon; speak from there. Hold your hand on your stomach to help your mind and body focus on it. See how you feel when speaking that way.

Wondering what to say? Make it easy on yourself and use an affirmation so you have something ready when practicing. When it's the same thing every time, you keep your brain focused on one thing at a time rather than being worried about the words you're using.

Exaggerate your breath and speak loudly to practice, continuing to keep your hand on your stomach. In fact, what you may think is loud isn't at all. This is why I recommend recording yourself and playing it back so you can adjust accordingly.

To start out with making the connection between your breath and your diaphragm, take a deep breath in and then, with your teeth together and your tongue against them, push bursts of air out of your mouth, keeping your hand on your stomach. That's a great way to start with recognizing the diaphragm.

VOCAL VARIETY

No one wants to listen to a monotone voice. Or a robotic voice. This is a surefire way to lose people. In order to be engaging and keep people's attention, you need to have vocal variety. Change up the volume, pitch, and cadence. You need to show interest in what you're saying, otherwise, people will tune out. Think about your voice as a roller coaster: highs, lows, and right across the middle. Put emphasis on certain words: speak with vocal punch every once in a while. Allow silence occasionally through a well-timed pause. Keep people on the edge of their seats.

SPEAK WITH PUNCTUATION

What will help engagement is something we don't think about very often: punctuating our speech. And by speech, I mean whenever you talk.

My clients ask, "How do I know when to pause?"

Imagine writing an email. Without even thinking, you punctuate your sentences. When we speak, the same should be true—to punctuate, yet somehow punctuation goes out the window. We end up with run-on sentences.

Most introductions are that way. People don't know what they want to say and sometimes even run out of words or trail off at the end because they haven't planned it. I'm always struck by how unprepared people are for introductions when life requires us to do it all the time (more on that in Chapter 4).

Usually, we attach one sentence fragment to the other, and therefore it doesn't sound polished (we end up sounding unsure and hesitant).

PART OF SPEAKING WITH CONFIDENCE IS SIMPLY TO SPEAK IN SENTENCES: HAVE APPROPRIATE COMMAS AND PERIODS—THAT'S WHEN YOU PAUSE.

Sometimes longer if you want a little drama.

Pausing is important to show control, and when things are in control, there is more trust and calm. If you're in control, your audience is going to feel at ease. That directly connects to your leadership presence and confidence.

If they're at ease, they're going to be much more open and able to listen to what you have to say.

The benefits of pausing are many:

- Replaces filler words
- Shows control = trust + leadership
- Adds anticipation and drama
- Lets the audience absorb what was said

- Gives us space to breathe
- Aids in slowing down
- Creates more vocal variety

POWER OF THE PAUSE

I remember working with a client who said—before we played his presentation video back—that he already knew he had lots of "um's." He even tallied them when on phone calls. That was a first. Part of the problem with that is that he was expecting them—even planning for them—so he actually sabotaged himself.

FILLER WORDS ARE A COMMON PROBLEM AND CAN HIJACK AN ENTIRE PRESENTATION OR HINDER A BUSINESS RELATIONSHIP.

They definitely affect whether or not people want to listen to you.

What's your most common one?

Um? Ah? Ya' know? Right? So? And um? Basically? Actually? Literally?

For me, it's "so." At one point, I was using a word combo: "The reality is..." and thankfully, a colleague of mine noticed and gave me that feedback. I had no awareness of that! That's why we need feedback. We have to ask for it.

When said excessively, any word or combination of words will distract from your message and your credibility.

When presenting this concept to a team at a Fortune 500 company, they exclaimed, "You need to help our boss! He always says, 'At the end of the day...'" Well, months later, I was back, and a senior leader was giving me a tour of the office. Sure enough, he said, "At the end of the day..." and I thought, "It's *you!*"

Both real words and non-words can be filler words.

It's especially fun when people combine them—like "and, so" and "and, um."

Here's how to get rid of filler words:

1. Be aware you're doing it

2. Get feedback in two ways

    a) Record yourself and play it back - as much as possible in a real-life situation. That will give you the most accurate feedback.
    b) Ask others for input: Do they hear it? It could be more excessive than you think, or the opposite may be true.

3. Use an affirmation: I am a person who perfectly pauses.

LET'S REMEMBER: WHEN YOU'RE SPEAKING, A PAUSE FEELS LIKE A LIFETIME, AND YET FOR THE AUDIENCE, IT FEELS NATURAL.

They barely even notice. In fact, if it's a well-timed pause or a pause to use silence instead of a filler word, it was actually effective (and strategic). We have to remember that when we speak, it's about our audience, not about us. It's about giving them the best experience.

Once when I was presenting this concept at a workshop, someone asked me to demonstrate the pause. I paused because I had to think about that for a moment. Then, I realized—he didn't even notice because I didn't have filler words. I was pausing as part of my punctuated speech, and therefore there were no distractions.

What I did instead was demonstrate what I *would've* sounded like had I *had* filler words based on what I had been teaching. For example, "Next, ah, we're going to um, focus, on, um, ah, ya' know, the power of um—ah—pausing."

Immediately the entire crowd reacted. "Oh my gosh!!! I see now. *Wow*, that's different."

SHOWS CONTROL = TRUST + LEADERSHIP

Think about when you're listening to someone. If they're using filler words and talking super fast or the opposite—

halting such that they sound tentative, it comes across as if they aren't in control. When people seem out of control, even slightly, they appear less trustworthy and not in charge. If it seems as if they aren't taking us somewhere, then we don't see them as a leader.

Mind you, this isn't usually something conscious. It's an impression we're left with, and we make a decision about them quickly.

You don't want to miss any opportunities because of a blind spot you have.

Imagine you're in a meeting, and someone is halting their speech. That's when we feel like we may need to interject to help move things along, or we tune out, or we keep pretending to listen, but our mind is somewhere else.

Adds anticipation and drama

Bond. [Pause]. James Bond. He's a perfect example of the dramatic pause. We can all hear this in our heads (if you've seen one of the movies or ads). Imagine if there were no pause in between. It would completely take away the gravitas in the statement. In a business setting, you may want to use it before unveiling something like, "The numbers in Q3 were beyond our wildest dreams [pause]: 25 million in revenue!"

It's a wonderful tool to have at your disposal to create anticipation. It often comes after a flagging statement (one in which you're setting the stage for what's coming next. It signifies something important or noteworthy will be said).

This creates more engagement as people are curious. The more you can leverage their curiosity, the more attentive they will be.

LETS THE AUDIENCE ABSORB WHAT WAS SAID

Often we talk so fast that we don't give the audience a chance to hear what was said because we're going at the speed of light, and people can't keep up. They don't *want* to keep up because it takes too many calories (thank you, Donald Miller, CEO of StoryBrand).

People need space to take in what you're saying. *You* know what you want to say and where you're headed, but the audience doesn't. Pause to give them a moment.

GIVES THE SPEAKER SPACE TO BREATHE

When a speaker talks fast they may mumble or slur their words, or they simply don't stop to breathe. We find ourselves wondering when they will take a breath. Or, when they finally do stop, they have to take a huge breath, and it is super obvious that they're nervous.

You want your audience focused on your content, not wondering if you're going to be okay!

AIDS IN SLOWING DOWN

Another reason to pause—pacing ourselves is important so our cadence is not too fast and not too slow, but just right.

CREATES MORE VOCAL VARIETY

This is one of the best and unsaid parts of the power of pausing—by simply pausing occasionally, that creates more variety along with your volume, pace, and pitch.

UPSPEAK BE GONE: SPEAK WITH DECLARATION

Upspeak, or Uptalk, is a slang term for when we say a statement as a question, making us sound tentative, hesitant, and unsure = lack of credibility.

It's such a different experience when people end their statements with a period because we sound significantly more confident.

If we spoke with punctuation, this wouldn't be an issue, but unfortunately, it happens to the best of us. It's a habit that we can change with intention and feedback, so don't lose heart!

Most of us are completely unaware that we're even doing it. This is why we need to record ourselves to see how we sound.

95% OF THE INTRODUCTIONS YOU HEAR ARE FILLED WITH UPSPEAK. THINK OF IT THIS WAY —MOST INTROS ARE RUN ON SENTENCES.

We say things like: "Hi? I'm Karen Laos? And I'm originally from Minnesota? But now I live in San Francisco? And before that I...."

You'd never write like that, so why do we speak like that?

Habit. The point is not to psychoanalyze the "why" but to fix it.

Instead of a questioning tone, be declarative instead. Say what you mean with conviction, as if you know what you're talking about.

There's a great scene in The Emperor's Club with Kevin Kline as a boys' prep school teacher. On the first day of class, he tells everyone to go around the room and state their name. The fourth kid ends up being an example to the class. When he says his name, it comes out as a question, and the teacher nails him for it: "Is that a question?"

Believe it or not, many people have a hard time saying their name with a period. UnitedHealthcare, one of my clients, has an executive development program where I prepare teams of six over six months to present to their executives. I spend a fair amount of time coaching them on saying their names with conviction when they come up to the stage. It's a common problem!

Another way to practice eliminating upspeak is to read a few sentences from a book out loud and record it. It can be any content. The point is to hear how your voice sounds different when punctuating.

When working with clients, I suggest they think about landing the plane. Where is this sentence going? Where am I landing this point? While that is often more to do with content, the same holds true for tone. If you can become aware of where you want to end, you can get there and land with conviction. Practice and see the difference!

I hear a lot of people say, "I love listening to you talk," or "No wonder you're a speaker." It's the best compliment I could get. I've worked diligently on my craft, and I'm glad it's noticed because that's what I've spent most of my life perfecting. When people bring that up, it reminds me that I don't even think about it anymore. It's ingrained in me.

That's what I want for you, too! People who speak with confidence get the promotions, the jobs, the gigs, the business—it's a humongous advantage!

Speak with a declarative tone like you mean it.

DITCH THE SCRIPT: BE CONVERSATIONAL

This is a big one! So many people rely on scripts. I'm not against notes, but I'm against what happens to most of us when we use a script: we read it, and then it sounds like we're reading. No one wants to listen to a robot or someone fake. That's usually how we sound when we script it out.

PEOPLE CONNECT HUMAN TO HUMAN. WE DON'T CONNECT WITH SOMEONE READING TO US.

Connection is the number one skill to have in life, as everything stems from that.

Are you familiar with "presentation mode?" This erodes credibility. That's the persona we fall into sometimes when presenting. I see this all the time. You're talking to a speaker before they get on stage, and suddenly on stage, they're a completely different person.

Be your conversational self. This can be extremely hard to do when we're so used to viewing a presentation as something formal. Society has taught us that we need to show up or be a certain way when we present.

When people are confusing and inconsistent, they are less credible. We also don't trust them as much because we're unsure who they are.

One thing I've learned in working with C-suite executives is that they notice an unnecessary formality when employees present to them—these employees forget that the C-suite leaders are people, too. I recognize there can be nervousness and a high-stakes feel in these cases, but if we prep and are so familiar with the material that we can be our conversational selves while presenting, this will serve us extremely well.

HOW TO PRESENT WITH NOTES

Here's what I recommend instead of a script: use Post-its with keywords. Put one point per post-it, and you can even draw a visual like a stick figure to quickly glance down and then come back to the audience. This allows you to speak from the heart. It's also very convenient to aid you in pausing. Look down at your notes while pausing.

Be your conversational self and still convey the information needed. Use minimal slides with most of them being visuals, when possible. Remember: you know the information better than you think.

And what happens if you script it out and lose your place? That's the worst! Then it's totally obvious that you were reading! And sometimes people even say "I'm sorry," or they go back and re-read—ugh! Avoid that at all costs.

PEOPLE WILL TRUST YOU MORE IF YOU CONNECT HUMAN TO HUMAN, AND THAT HAPPENS THROUGH A CONVERSATIONAL TONE.

MORE ON TONE

One of the issues with women, in particular, is coming across with a breathy tone. This is another good example of how we can come across differently than who we are when we're simply having a conversation with others. We get into this higher resonance tone, and it sounds overly dramatic or simply less credible because it's too airy, and people associate credibility with a deeper tone.

Remember to use your breath to support your tone. Pause to breathe and focus on your diaphragm to leverage strength in your voice.

I've also noticed women tend to get higher in pitch when nervous. We want to stay—at a minimum—in our regular vocal tone, not higher. Then it seems like we're nervous.

IT ALL COMES BACK TO CREDIBILITY: PEOPLE TRUST US MORE WHEN WE'RE OUR NATURAL, AUTHENTIC SELVES RATHER THAN SOMEONE WHO SHOWS UP DIFFERENTLY WHEN PRESENTING OR LEADING A MEETING.

What about you? What's the one thing you could do to make your voice stand out this week?

4

LEADERSHIP PRESENCE

When asked to define leadership presence, an executive vice president once said, "I don't know how to define it, but I know it when I see it."

Isn't that the truth? It's hard to define it. Some people call it polish, gravitas, charisma, you name it, but how can we define it enough to know how to *be* it?

My goal is to take out the mystery. After working with clients on elevating their presence for the past 20+ years, experience has taught me that there are tangible behaviors we can learn that demonstrate presence which then translate to influence and impact.

The good news is that it's a skill you can learn. Many people believe that you are born with it, and you're out of luck if you're not.

The challenge? Like anything, it takes intention, practice, feedback, and support.

In a nutshell, the four components of leadership presence are:

1. Connection (eye contact)

2. Credibility (posture, pausing)

3. Energy (voice, movement, gestures)

4. Likability (facial expression)

The key is knowing how to map each of the above components to behaviors that actually demonstrate these.

How do you build trust and credibility quickly?

What do you actually *do*?

WHAT LEADERSHIP PRESENCE LOOKS LIKE

The combo of these four components gives us leadership presence. There is crossover between them, too—likability can also be determined by vocal tone along with facial expressions. My point is, no need to get caught up in a formula. They are integrated. Work on one of these at a time to build up to all of them for the whole package.

At a glance, leadership presence is looking people in the eye with a smile, so they feel a connection to you. It's a strong handshake and standing up straight. It's speaking like you know what you're talking about, projecting your voice loud enough so people can hear you. It's not being tentative or halting in your speech—as if you don't know what you're talking about.

It's pausing to show control.

It's using your hands in a way that illuminates what you're saying, rather than keeping them stuck in a handclasp or shrugging your shoulders inward and not expanding your hands.

It's standing up straight.

People trust someone more with these characteristics.

It's unfair but true.

If two people interview for a job or two go after the same business, one might have less experience than the other, but if the other is the better communicator, most likely, that person will be picked.

If you're building your skills in this area, beware of words that are up for interpretation:

animated, passionate, and energetic, for example. When facilitating groups on presence, I do lots of video recording and playback. Many times participants will give feedback to others, saying, "You had lots of passion."

I'm in the business of making everything tangible so it can be replicated. What does "passion" mean? How do you define it? I always challenge people by asking, "What did they do in their presentation that made you know they were passionate? What behavior did they demonstrate? Once we get to that, then we're getting somewhere.

Passion often comes across in a strong voice, a smile, and a forward lean with our posture. Right there, you've got three elements to replicate! The more specific you can get with your behaviors, the easier it will be to make the changes you desire.

RESEARCH SAYS

Albert Mehrabian did a study back in 1967 that continues to be referenced from a credibility standpoint for anything related to communication and presentation. He wanted to find out what held the most weight when communicating. He brought to light that there are always three components to a message.

The surprise for most of us is how they play out percentage-wise. Here they are:

1. Vocal (how you sound) 38%

2. Visual (what people see of you) 55%

3. Verbal (what you're saying—the words themselves) 7%

Are you surprised by the verbal holding only 7% weight?

What's important to know is what this doesn't mean. It doesn't mean that only 7% of what you say matters. These numbers relate to an inconsistent message. When the words you say don't match the way you come across. For example, if I say "I'm excited," and I do it with a frown and look down, your brain immediately registers it as inconsistent and only hears 7% of the message.

Isn't the verbal where we spend most of our time when preparing for an important meeting or presentation? I've never had a client come to me saying they have a nervous twitch or that they do something weird with their face when presenting. Everyone comes to me with their message asking if it flows, is organized, makes sense, etc. We're so concerned about our content. I get it!

HERE'S THE PROBLEM: WE NEED TO RECOGNIZE THAT AS HUMANS, WE ARE WIRED AS EMOTIONAL BEINGS. WE JUDGE QUICKLY. WE DECIDE WITHIN NANOSECONDS IF WE WANT TO KEEP LISTENING TO SOMEONE OR NOT.

Much of that decision is based on how we come across.

CONNECTION: EYE CONTACT

We build connection through our eyes. From the moment we enter the world, we immediately look into our mother's or caregiver's eyes. It's a foundational human behavior and need.

That's why it feels so odd when someone you're talking to is looking down or away (maybe looking over your shoulder for the more "interesting" person to talk to!). At our core, we need connection, and it starts with our eyes.

If you're not looking people in the eye or your eyes are darting around the room, you may appear:

- Untrustworthy.
- Nervous
- As if you don't know what you're talking about.

Lots of reasons to have solid eye contact.

When speaking to an audience, most presenters look at people for 1-2 seconds, if that. They're mostly darting around the room, favoring one side of the room, or looking up at the ceiling as a habit. They may be scanning the room, but they're not actually connecting.

When presenting, instead of the one to two second average of eye contact per person, you want to reach three to four seconds per person.

Too often, a presenter will think, "Oh, I have to look at everybody, so I'm going to scan the room back and forth," like a tennis match, for example, yet that's not how people connect.

They connect person to person, so it may seem weird at first to you when you're the presenter, and you're looking at somebody for three or four seconds, but to the receiver, it actually creates the optimal level of connection.

Let's take a 1:1 conversation, for example. On average, we would look at each other for about seven to 10 seconds before one of us would look away because if we were looking any longer than that, it would be awkward.

When you translate that 1:1 experience of natural connection to an audience setting (two or more people), then holding eye contact for three to four seconds will make you come across as confident and in control.

CREDIBILITY (POSTURE, PAUSING)

The more space we take up, the more power we're perceived to have. What's fun about that is we don't even have to possess power or have confidence, but we come across that way.

Posture is key.

How you walk into a room physically or show up in that Zoom room matters. Own it.

Stand or sit tall with your shoulders back. Take up space.

Expand your elbows away from your body. Unclasp your hands and have an open posture. Too often, we make ourselves physically smaller, keeping our hands closed, our shoulders in, our elbows in, and we cross our legs.

If you're standing, make sure you're standing solidly on both feet with your weight evenly distributed. You want to look strong, grounded, and unwavering. Avoid leaning on one leg. That's a passive stance.

These shifts are subtle but make a difference.

LIKE MANY CONCEPTS OF PRESENCE, IT'S A BUNCH OF SUBTLETIES THAT ADD UP TO AN IMPRESSION PEOPLE ARE LEFT WITH.

We then make a judgment from that. For better or worse, it's what we do. Therefore, you want to project the best version of yourself.

Dr. Amy Cuddy (Social Psychologist) made the Power Pose famous. Be sure to watch her TED talk. The gist is to stand or sit in a pose like Wonder Woman for two minutes. Notice how you feel more confident when you do this. Tip: do it in the bathroom before an important meeting or presentation.

Pausing is covered in Chapter 3, but it's important to call out as part of credibility.

ENERGY (VOICE, MOVEMENT, GESTURES)

We cover Voice in Chapter 3 but remember it's a big contributor to both credibility and energy.

MOVEMENT

With movement comes energy, and with energy comes engagement. The key is to move with purpose. Take a few steps, and then plant yourself in place for a little while. Then move again to a different part of the room. Use as much of the room as possible while avoiding side stepping, shifting weight, and dancing (unless, of course, there's music).

One of the biggest problems is the lack of purposeful movement. The result is nervousness and uncertainty, and a lack of credibility.

Eye contact and movement go together well. Look at someone in the audience as you walk toward them. Stay in one place, looking at a few people (3-4 seconds each), and then move again.

WHEN USING A PODIUM, ONE OF THE BIGGEST MISTAKES PEOPLE MAKE IS TO STAND DIRECTLY BEHIND IT.

That only creates a barrier between you and your audience. Do your best to either move it to the side (it's amazing how a slight shift makes a massive difference), or if it's immovable, stand beside it and move around the room, only coming back to it for referencing your notes.

If it's immovable *and* you need it for the microphone, do what one of my clients did. When she spoke, she stood behind it but walked toward the audience when they were asking questions. Whatever you can do to prevent the barrier so you're more connected to people.

GESTURES

People often ask, "What do I do with my hands!" I suggest using them to illuminate your content (naturally, like you're talking with friends and you're not even thinking about it) and then resting them at your sides. That can be the hardest part, but it makes you look the most in control and open. My approximation of the ideal formula is to use your hands about 70% of the time and spend the other 30% resting (goes hand in hand with the pause).

With gestures, sometimes people don't know how to start. We do it naturally and don't even think about it, but once we're thinking about it, we feel ill equipped to know what to do!

Think about expanding your arms, in general, to take up more space.

When you've got something to share that's quantifiable, you could say, "There are two things I want to share." While saying this, you could put your hand straight above your head with two fingers demonstrating the two things.

Intentionally get your elbow away from your body to create more impact versus keeping it stuck to your body.

The general rule of thumb is to go big with your gestures. Then put your hands at your sides when not using them.

TOO OFTEN, WE PUT OUR HANDS IN FRONT OF US CLASPED OR IN THE FIG LEAF POSITION (HANDS DOWN IN FRONT OF US AND ON TOP OF EACH OTHER). THIS ONLY MAKES US LOOK SMALLER, PASSIVE, AND WEAK.

One of my best client stories is from a leader who had a hard time unclasping his hands in front of his body. He kept saying, "I have to get my hands to break up with each other, but they keep wanting to get back together!"

Be intentional about using your hands with gestures that would be appropriate to the content that you're talking about.

When seated in a meeting, present with your hands above the table. When you're not using them, rest your wrists slightly above the edge of the table, hip-width apart. In other words, don't clasp or put your hands in front of your body. You will appear more open and approachable this way.

At AT&T in San Ramon, CA, an executive leader wanted to introduce me and my talk. She asked if I would record her and give her feedback later. It was fascinating. At the beginning of her intro, her hands were stuck under the table as she was gesturing, so it looked like she was trapped. Shortly thereafter, her hands came above the table, and it made a world of difference in her presence.

LIKABILITY (FACIAL EXPRESSION)

YOUR SMILE IS THE BRIDGE TO LIKABILITY, CONNECTION, AND WARMTH.

If you smile, you're going to come across as more approachable, open, and friendly. People like likable people!

Remember: It's all about your "know, like, and trust factor."

CONNECTION OVER PERFECTION

The importance of connection over perfection became real for me in 2006 when I was learning a new corporate training program and had been studying hard for months. My task was to deliver the modules in front of my boss, the company president (no pressure!), so she could sign off on me being ready to deliver in front of clients.

After presenting to her, I excitedly anticipated her praise. What came next was a massive surprise. She said, "Well, if I really listen, the content was practically perfect. But you looked angry the whole time!" Apparently I had a furrowed brow during the entire presentation.

In shock, I took note. It took me a while to process because I'm such a fun-loving person who smiles and laughs easily, but clearly not when presenting material I was concentrating on like crazy. It was then that I realized the power of the smile during a presentation.

After 20 some years of coaching now, I've come to realize that I wasn't alone. Most people have a more serious face when presenting *unless* they're intentionally thinking about it. You don't have to be smiling the whole time; that could be inauthentic and take away trust. But, you want to have a lightness about your expression that shows approachability. Otherwise, it will be very hard for people to connect with you.

Some people ask: "What if I'm giving a serious presentation? I want to be taken seriously. Why would I smile then?" This goes back to having a lightness of face and expressing the appropriate emotion for what's being said. It's about variety in your facial expressions. Raising your eyebrows can be a way to accomplish something similar to a smile.

The problem is that we're always contending with the concept of disparity. There's usually a gap between how we think we're coming across and how we actually are coming across.

For example, in this case, most people think their expressions are okay (let's face it; most of us aren't thinking about it that much—we're thinking about our content, if people like what we're saying, if we're making sense, if we look good, etc.).

YOU CAN'T SACRIFICE CONNECTION FOR PERFECTION.

For those wondering where to smile while presenting, another great rule of thumb is to do it during the benefits that you're offering to your audience. I always say, if you think of nowhere else to do it, do it when you first begin speaking or at the benefits.

Another example from my life is at the airport. Ever had a delayed flight? Before I knew about the true power of having a light expression, I would approach the agents, and sometimes their expression was unfriendly even as I approached. My epiphany was that I was approaching them with a sour expression, so they were reacting to my expression unintentionally, and it didn't feel good to either party.

Going back to the power of the experience you create, I was creating a bad experience simply because of my face! I started catching on that when I would remember to have a light expression as I spoke, the result was very different. Maybe not always 100% positive because of the issue, but the interaction was much better, and I'd have a much better chance of influencing them to get me on that next flight.

Smile more than you think you need to. As soon as we get serious for too long, your audience feels less engaged and connected. In most communications, even when serious, there's a place for the positive or at least for hope. For example, if you said, "There are a million children dying in the world," of course you're going to be more serious, but then you can transition to (with a smile) "....but there's hope and if you donate to this organization here's what your money will do."

LEADERSHIP IS CONSISTENCY

Many years back, I was about to facilitate a corporate training on presentation skills. As I greeted people walking into the room, one of the participants shook my hand, and my immediate impression was, "This guy is going to be challenging." Simply because of his facial expression.

He came across as unfriendly and almost a little intimidating. It turns out he was a nice guy with a great sense of humor. When we played back the video recording of his presentation, we looked at it together, and he said, "Whoa! I look so rude and intimidating." I said, "I know, that's exactly what I thought of you when I met you this morning!" I would've never said that had he not seen his video. His seeing that for himself was the connection.

I could've told him directly, but the power came in his own discovery. The bigger "aha" for him was that how he was coming across didn't represent his personality. I said, "I agree. My first impression of you was very different from how you actually are."

His big takeaway: "I've got to intentionally smile so that I bring out my personality when I meet people, especially for the first time. The same thing goes for how I am around my team. I don't want them to think I'm intimidating or rude."

FOLLOW THE 80/20 RULE

While we can't be perfect, here's a way to think about it: follow the 80/20 rule. If we can focus on demonstrating these concepts 80% of the time and allowing ourselves grace the other 20% of the time, we'll be much farther along than most. This goes for all of the concepts of leadership presence.

VIRTUAL PRESENCE

Eye contact

Eye contact in the virtual world is tricky. To this date, it presents the biggest challenge for me personally. Often we look at ourselves, or we look at where the audience is from our perspective.

Where we need to be looking is the webcam (technically, you want to be looking about an inch or centimeter below the green dot so that it appears that you're looking at them).

Most likely, the person to whom you're speaking will be somewhere else on your screen other than where the webcam is. Perhaps they're on the bottom or to the side. Therefore, if you're looking where it's comfortable for you (at them), they're going to have the experience that you're looking away. We have to remember that.

IT'S NOT ABOUT YOU. IT'S ABOUT YOUR LISTENER. LOOK AT THE WEBCAM.

As hard as that can sometimes be (I get it: we want to see their facial expressions so we can connect), looking at the webcam ensures that they feel a connection with you. This increases trust and makes you look focused and confident.

It's about the audience's experience of us and what their impression is. It all connects back to whether they trust us, whether they like us, and whether they think we're credible.

PHYSICALITY
Zoom framing: Center yourself in the frame and make sure to avoid wasted space above your head. The frame's job is to highlight you, so place the top of the computer frame at

the top of your head, and ideally distance yourself enough from the screen so you can be viewed waist up.

This will enable you to show your hands. Using gestures creates more energy which will engage your audience.

Another way to influence and show engagement occasionally is to physically lean in.

Want more on Virtual Presentations? Here are 10 Tips:

DON'T DRAW ATTENTION TO MISTAKES

If you make a mistake, remember that the audience isn't paying that close attention. Most people aren't even going to notice.

Try one of these two things:

Pause for a second to gather your thoughts. If you're pausing throughout your whole talk already, it won't be a big deal to the audience because it will be a part of your cadence. You don't want to show it on your face. Stop, pause, gather your thoughts and continue on.

If you make a mistake that is blatantly obvious to everybody, say something quickly like, "Excuse me," or "I was off on that one," or "I'll come back and rectify that." You don't have to fall on the sword and pontificate about how bad you feel or profusely apologize. Solve the problem and move on quickly.

It's always a judgment call to decide: is this something I actually need to acknowledge, or can I just move on?

During my workout at the gym once, there was apparently a tech problem. The workout is choreographed with music while we're on a treadmill. The instructor kept talking about the tech, "Oh, I'm sorry for these mistakes."

All I'm focused on is getting a workout. I would have never known the difference, nor did I care. She didn't have to keep bringing up the mistake.

Then what happens is, when we call attention to it, our audience starts focusing on it: "Oh, she did make a mistake. I wonder if she's going to make another one. Maybe she isn't so credible. Maybe this isn't as good as I thought it was," and we start doubting the person themselves.

Avoid that by simply moving on.

YOU CONTROL THE EXPERIENCE

Something we don't think about much is that we're always giving people an experience of us when they're in our presence. The question is, is it a good one or not? Do people feel drawn toward us, drawn away from us, or is it more of a neutral experience? In other words, are we memorable? And if so, what for?

In my client work, I always invite people to think about this. I love posing the questions: "How do you want people to feel in your presence? or "How do you want people to talk about you when you leave the room?" and "What do you want to be known for as a leader?"

If you start with these questions, you have the foundation of how you want to come across.

You have more control than you think.

If you want to influence, you need to create good experiences. For example, if I'm presenting in a meeting, I have control over my voice. I have control over my ability to smile or not. I have control over my hand gestures, posture, and so on.

If you want to make an impact, what impact do you want to make?

Obviously we can't control how somebody receives us, but we can do everything in our power to come across in a way that best represents us.

I've heard my whole life that people feel comfortable around me. I've had several people tell me things that they say they've never told anyone else; that they feel comfortable sharing and opening up.

It wasn't until I was in business that I realized how powerful that was. It's been a point of differentiation for me in my career. The term psychological safety is now something I realize I've been creating all along. That makes me feel good, too—knowing that I can be a safe person for people.

We also have the power to create bad experiences.

In London on a business trip, my husband witnessed me creating a less than desirable experience for someone. Yikes.

Chris rarely travels with me for business, but he was on the sidelines as I approached what I thought was a security guard at the hotel. I wanted to know which way to leave the building to see Big Ben. I had been waiting in line at the concierge desk where there was a long line of people and had grown impatient. I left the line and walked up to the supposed security guard, "Can you tell me which way to leave the hotel to see Big Ben?" He said, "I don't work here." I was so frustrated because I had already been waiting a long time in line, and it was such a simple question. Exasperated, I said, "What is your role here anyway?"

Not my best moment!

My husband said, "That was so rude, did you hear yourself?" I was really embarrassed and felt so guilty for being a jerk!

I could have controlled that to play out very differently. I could have smiled and said in a friendly tone, "My apologies! I thought you worked here." That would have been a very different experience, and I would have looked a lot better to him, as well.

This is such a good example of how we can portray ourselves in a way that does not project who we really are. That one experience I gave was bad, and if he saw me again, he probably wouldn't want to interact with me.

In gratitude, I write that we don't have to be defined by one moment in time. It's about consistency. If you think about good leadership, it's about the moments that add up over time where the person's character shows up.

Let's remember: people judge quickly, so you want to put forth your best self whenever possible. Don't give people space to create evidence against you when it's in your power to do otherwise.

5

CONFUSION TO CLARITY: HOW TO STOP RAMBLING AND GET TO THE POINT

Our tendency to ramble is one of the biggest obstacles to presenting well. As a recovering rambler myself, I get it. It's hard to stay on point when we have so much to say, or we're nervous. Sometimes we come across as unfocused without realizing it. Or, we realize it and have a hard time knowing how to get out of it.

As Donald Miller (CEO of StoryBrand) says, "If you confuse, you lose." If people have to burn too many calories to figure out what you're trying to say, they'll tune you out.

Start by making sure you have a point in the first place. What is the lead of your story? What do you most want the audience to know? What is the main idea that frames the rest of your message? Another Donald Miller-ism: what is your "controlling idea?"

State that upfront.

Too often, here's what happens: you start delivering information, and it's a data dump. Information overload with no direction.

I was coaching a senior vp in compliance on presenting to her new board of directors. We began with practicing her presentation. As I hit record, she launched into the information with no real context or direction. Instead of "Here are the numbers we'll be going over," which is purely informational, say, "We had significant revenue growth in Q3 over Q2." The second one offers a point of view that gives the talk direction.

THE CURSE OF KNOWLEDGE

This happens all the time. People launch into their talk with an assumption that the audience is in their heads or knows as much as they do. Enter the Curse of Knowledge. The more expert we are in our field, the harder it is to see things through the lens of our audience. The truth is, we often don't even realize it. We jump in with what we want to say and hope it lands.

OUR JOB IS TO TRANSLATE THE KNOWLEDGE IN OUR HEADS TO THE AUDIENCE IN A WAY THAT'S UNDERSTANDABLE, RELATABLE, AND MEMORABLE.

Most of us are trying to prove ourselves, so we're so consumed with getting it right and looking good. It's a natural human instinct. In fact, I used to be a leadership consultant at Gap Inc, and a concept that has always struck me from my days there is in a book called the *Knowing-Doing Gap* (no pun intended!) by Pfeffer and Sutton out of Stanford. In the research of the authors, they realized that we as human beings are committed to these three things, above all else: Looking good, Being Right, and Being in Control.

What an insightful tip on human behavior! This has helped me be more aware of my own behavior, but especially of others'. For example, it gives me more compassion for people when I see them "peacocking" or being overly perfectionistic. I usually think, "Ah, she's just trying to look good right now." Or "He wants to be right. That's all it is."

The Curse of Knowledge is also when we use jargon or buzzwords that people don't understand. For example, I had a physical injury a few years ago, and the doctor kept saying, "The calcaneus this, the calcaneus that," and after several minutes, I finally said, "What's the calcaneus?"

He said, "Oh, it's your heel bone." That's when I said to myself, "I wish I had known that when you first started talking, Doc." Too often, we don't take time to think about who our audience is and what matters to them and adjust our message appropriately.

This desire to prove ourselves makes us feel like we need to convince someone and share all that we know or have done.

THE TRUTH IS, WE DON'T NEED MORE CONTENT. WHAT WE NEED IS SIMPLICITY—FOCUS INSTEAD OF FUMBLING.

More doesn't make it better. And worse, more without direction makes it almost tragic. Or certainly self-sabotage. You don't want to lose people when you're in full control of the experience.

Be Brief. Be Bright. Be Done.

The goal is to have a point, land it and move on."Be brief, be bright, be done."

Here's another example of the data dump:

On two different calls recently, people were sharing information with me that was more detailed than I needed.

Too much detail can not only tune people out but can be overwhelming in spite of how important it might be to you. We have to think about our audience's needs.

If you start with the point or the reason you're sharing the information, that is a wonderful way to introduce the content that's coming.

Before you share information, ask yourself, what is the reason I'm sharing this? How will it serve my listener?

Bonus: another wonderful way to engage with someone to see if they need all of that is to ask what would be helpful for them to know. That can steer the conversation in a more focused direction.

Let's get back to rambling. How do you fix it? Here are two ways:

1. If you notice yourself doing it and your words are already out there, pause, gather your thoughts and say out loud, "My point is this..." and state your point.

2. If you realize you're lost, pause, stay silent, gather your thoughts and move on with your point or the next part of your talk. No one will notice the difference, most likely. Pausing gives the audience a chance to absorb what you said and gives their brains a break.

BOTTOM LINE UP FRONT

BLUF is an acronym that stands for Bottom Line Up Front, a term from the U.S. military to make communication precise and powerful. State your point up front so you don't lose the listener.

KNOW YOUR AUDIENCE

Avoiding the Curse of Knowledge gets you one step closer to having a message of influence. There are questions I'd recommend you ask yourself when preparing for a meeting or a talk.

Questions such as:

What does your audience care about? (this can be a humbling one sometimes. They may not care about what you want to focus on!).

I see this a lot in sales pitches. For example, I was coaching an architecture firm on their pitch, and it was fairly typical. Beautiful slides in the beginning of the deck showcasing how great they are. I understand. Again, we want to prove ourselves; show all of our accolades and why the client should choose us.

The problem? They were starting with themselves. This is the biggest blunder with a pitch or any message of influence, really.

WHAT DO PEOPLE CARE ABOUT? THEMSELVES! THIS IS WHY WE MUST FOCUS ON THEM FIRST.

What do *they* want to know? What matters to them?

Start by asking those questions to get clear on where to focus your message. Then craft your point from there.

WHAT'S YOUR POINT?

When coaching a senior leader many years back at Genentech, the large biotech in South San Francisco, I had a memorable experience that demonstrated the power of having a point up front.

She was looking to move internally at the company, so I was helping her with interview prep. We all know the standard interview question: "Tell me about yourself."

When I did the mock interview with her, I played the role of interviewer, and her answer to that question was a classic data dump of information with no direction.

I stopped her, asking her to think about her audience. "What does that interviewer care about? The interviewer likely has 2-4 other candidates that she's meeting, so she wants to know as quickly and efficiently as possible if you're the right fit.

What is the most important thing you want me, as the interviewer, to know about you?"

She said, "I love research, and I've got the experience you're looking for!"

My answer? "Great! Lead with that!"

On take two, she sounded much more focused and clear. There was a point up front, and all the details came after that. Much easier for the listener to process.

An alternate way to start might have been: "Before I get into the details, the most important thing for you to know about me is that I love research, and that's why I'm excited about this opportunity."

INVITE THEM TO ACTION

The other thing we want to do is give them an action to take. This is missed all too often in business.

WHAT I'VE OBSERVED IS IMPLIED ACTION, NOT A DIRECT ASK.

For example, when giving a pitch or simply a message of influence at work, here's what I hear at the end: "If you're interested..." which is a passive ask. It's a cop-out. Usually not a conscious one. I've had people swear to me that they included an action step when doing the pitch role play, but it's not until they see the video that they realize they didn't. Instead of the former, say instead: "Would you be interested in learning more?" or "Would you like to talk about the next steps?"

The reason we are not inclined to make a direct ask is because it's vulnerable. And, no one likes rejection. If you make a direct ask, you're expecting either a "yes" or a "no," and we always think the worst, so you're essentially expecting a no.

WHAT'S IN IT FOR THEM?

We all have that antenna above our heads that says, "What's in it for me?!" so as a presenter, we need to be attuned to that. What benefits could you share that will make the person buy off on what you're selling? Whether it's an idea or a product?

The key is to make the benefits as individually beneficial as possible. Avoid saying, "Your company will increase revenue..." Say instead, "You'll have more exposure to the board" or "You'll be seen as an influential leader." The more you can get to the heart of the person, the more likely they'll want to do what you want them to do.

AVOID THE PLEASANTRIES

Here's what not to do when beginning a presentation.

One of the biggest mistakes people make at the beginning of a presentation is having a bunch of words that don't mean much, such as "I'm so excited to be here, I'm thrilled to be here, it's great to be here, I can't wait to talk about, thank you for having me.

ALL OF THESE PLEASANTRIES WEAKEN THE IMPACT OF WHAT COULD BE A POWERFUL OPENING.

As humans, we're conditioned to say those things, and we're conditioned to hear them.

That's why, when you avoid using them, you stand out. Instead of using those pleasantries, start immediately with a story, anecdote, statistic, or quote. That will immediately grab attention and show the audience that you're worth listening to.

We have to earn the right to get the audience's attention. This is a powerful way to do that right from the beginning. We all know the drill: you don't get a second chance to make a first impression!

Sometimes people ask me, "When I start speaking, aren't I supposed to introduce myself?" Start with the story or the example first, and then introduce yourself.

PEOPLE DON'T REALLY CARE WHO YOU ARE, THEY CARE FIRST ABOUT BEING DRAWN IN AND DECIDING IF YOU'RE INTERESTING ENOUGH FOR THEM TO WANT TO LISTEN.

How are you capturing their attention?

START WITH A STORY

I was hired by a large energy company to coach three executives on their presentations to the Board. One gentleman stands out because he said, "What story can I possibly come up with? I'm just a numbers guy. I go up to the front of the room and talk through the Excel spreadsheet."

I said, "We've got to make this more interesting!" We started talking about his interests, and then he shared how much he loves sports.

Then it came to him: "I have the best idea!"

Here's what he did that was a huge hit: he started his presentation with a question.

"What's the first thing that you do when you walk into a sporting event? After you get your beer and your popcorn, what do you do when you get into your seat?

You look at the scoreboard. That's what we're doing today. We're looking at the scoreboard to show you how the company is doing."

It took effort to get there, but anything worth doing well is worth the effort. He stood out and was remembered.

If you start looking for examples to use, they are there. Be proactive, so when you *do* have to present or lead a meeting, you'll have a story ready.

USING SLIDES EFFECTIVELY

The data dump is alive and well in Powerpoint decks, even though when *we* watch a presentation, we don't want all of that detail on a slide and then someone reading it to us. Somehow, when we have to present, we load the deck with information!

Let's stop that. Keep it simple. Use visuals whenever possible (photos are fantastic) and animate your slides such that only one key point at a time is on each slide. You can build a slide with one point at a time to turn into a slide with five points at the end, for example.

If you want five questions to ask as you prepare to speak, scan the QR Code below:

6

SEIZE OPPORTUNITIES: SAY "YES" TO THE ADVENTURE

A dear childhood friend of mine says that I always seem to be in the right place at the right time. It feels like it because of the incredible experiences I've had.

Here's what I say: I pay attention.

Just a few weeks ago (as I write this on April 17, 2022), I had the opportunity to be published in a book with 16 other authors called *Invisible No More: Stepping into the Spotlight*. You know that feeling when you realize you're not alone?

The experience reminded me of how many people choose to be invisible. Or simply *don't* choose to be visible. There's a difference. Sometimes we keep ourselves hidden without even realizing it. We don't go for opportunities right in front of us because we either don't notice them or don't think we're qualified or good enough.

YOU ARE ALWAYS GOOD ENOUGH.

And what's the worst thing that can happen? It doesn't work out, and then you move on to the next possibility.

Remember the story in Chapter 2 when I didn't raise my hand for the speaking part I could've had? That's an example of staying hidden without realizing it. I had a split-second moment where I wanted to volunteer, but I didn't. I hesitated, and then it was too late.

You've got to seize them when they show up. Sometimes, you have to create them.

In 2002 I was tired of my Human Resources responsibilities in my corporate job, and I wanted to do what I loved: train and develop people. I decided to take a stab at creating a new role for myself and pitching it to my boss. I focused on the company's need for training and a person dedicated to that. I highlighted my gifts and skills that lend themselves to this new role. As another boss in my life used to say, "Make it impossible for me to say 'no.'" My pitch worked, and I became head of training for the San Francisco office.

Maybe there's something in your life that you want to change? How can you find an opportunity where it doesn't seem to exist? One of my favorite quotes is "Every wall is a door," by Ralph Waldo Emerson. It may not appear to be there, but perhaps you can create it.

SOMETIMES OPPORTUNITIES COME IN UNEXPECTED PACKAGES

I've been laid off three times, and each time has led to something bigger and better. The most significant layoff happened in 1998, where I had been an HR manager for an intercultural training company. The company folded as we put too much attention on one client (Hewlett Packard). When HP moved their business elsewhere, we tanked.

After leaving the office for the last time, I did my normal swim routine at the Embarcadero YMCA. While doing a lap engrossed in thought, it occurred to me. "I can do anything I want now!" Then, I chuckled at myself in the pool, "Karen, you can do anything you want anytime!" It happened to be a forced opportunity that would move me into a new role that opened up the door for more of what I love *and* at a higher level with more exposure.

It's now fun to look back and see how my journey has progressed.

How about you? What life lessons have you learned about seizing opportunities?

SAY "YES" TO THE INVITATION

Back to the *Invisible No More* book. I first met Hollis Citron through the Brainz Magazine Facebook Group in the Fall of 2021. She had put a post out looking for podcast guests. I jumped at the chance. After that, she invited me to be a contributing author in the book *Invisible No More*. She's also the one who published this book (that you're reading) for me!

BESIDES PAYING ATTENTION, SOMETIMES IT'S A MATTER OF SAYING "YES" TO AN INVITATION.

My mom used to say, "If you're invited to a party, just go!" When my dad passed away in 2007, my brother called Mom for a last-minute invitation to a theater performance. She said, "Yes! I'll go anywhere, anytime." She was always up for an adventure.

We can miss out on opportunities if we're constantly looking at the "what if" scenario. "What if I don't have a good time? What if I feel uncomfortable talking to people? What if I'm stuck there with no way out, and it's awkward to leave? What if it doesn't work out?"

What if we flipped it? "What if I have the time of my life? What if I meet someone amazing? What if I find out I have a new interest I never knew I had? What if I get a new business opportunity?"

EXPECT THE BEST, AND YOU'LL OFTEN GET IT.

That's my philosophy. It's all about how you look at it. Life is an adventure waiting for you!

The more we dive in headfirst, the more life we'll get to experience.

DO YOU WANT TO RIDE AN ELEPHANT?

Riding an elephant in Thailand after a 30-hour travel day and a spontaneous decision still remains one of the most exhilarating experiences of my life. I had facilitated a training in Malaysia the week prior, and one of the participants lived in Thailand. I exclaimed, "I'll be in Bangkok next week!"

That's how the beginning of my Bangkok tour was born. Before I knew it, he had emailed me with a potential itinerary.

After my arrival at the airport, his driver picked me up in a white van and brought me back to his office, where I met him briefly, and his staff whooshed me off for the tour.

He'd join me for the afternoon. The two HR women were giddy with excitement to host me and said, "Mr. J is rich! He gave us money to take you around." I was humbled and thrilled all at the same time! The van took off, and soon after, one of the HR women said, "Do you like coffee?" and next I know, we were in a coffee shop, and they said, "get whatever you want." It was like that all day. Thai massage, the King's Palace, a boat tour, and lunch in a pineapple on the river; it was a fairytale day that I will never forget.

I truly had no idea what was coming at every turn of the day. I was living it moment by moment.

My favorite part of the day was the elephant ride. But not for the reason that you'd expect. The ride itself was a cool experience, but the best part was beforehand.

Driving through the outer streets of Bangkok and unexpectedly and spontaneously hearing the question from one of my hosts, "Have you ever ridden an elephant?" as if it was a regular occurrence for most.

Suddenly, the van turned around, and I was soon in line to ride one of those beautiful creatures.

The value of being spontaneous is not to be underestimated. This isn't the first time this kind of thing has happened to me.

BEING OPEN TO NEW EXPERIENCES AND ADVENTURES IS IMPORTANT TO LIVING A FUN AND ABUNDANT LIFE!

But we have to show up. Where are you showing up in your life right now? Are you available?

ONE OF THE BIGGEST LESSONS I'VE LEARNED FROM OWNING A BUSINESS IS THE IMPORTANCE OF BEING SEEN. YOU DON'T WANT TO BE THE BEST-KEPT SECRET IN YOUR INDUSTRY.

People have to know you're available and understand what it is that you offer if you want them to choose you. This goes for a relationship or a business deal.

We have to show up and speak up.

SHOW UP

When I first left corporate in 2003 to start my own business, I jumped in headfirst. I had saved $10,000 to focus on my coaching business. Given my HR background, I began calling everyone I knew to tell them of my new venture.

I was great at showing up.

What I failed to do is have focus. I was great at connections and showing up, but I wasn't great at articulating what I do in a way that people knew how to refer clients to me.

MY PROBLEM

Here's what was on the bottom of my business card as my tagline that did *not* work: "Life, career, business coaching." How would anyone know what my focus was? I look back and laugh now, but isn't this what a lot of us do? We want to be as broad as possible to cast a wide net so we don't lose anyone out, and God forbid, lose business.

The problem? It's too broad, so there's no focus. When I started saying, "I work with women over 40 who are stressed out and depleted," that's when people would respond immediately and say, "That's me!"

We need first to identify who we want to work with and the problem that we solve.

Whether you're in a corporate role or a business owner, you're solving someone's problem. The key is to define the problem, share it, and communicate how you solve it. Not an easy task.

Most of us make assumptions and don't think about this when talking about what we do for a living.

WE LAUNCH INTO AN INFORMATIONAL MONOLOGUE, AND OTHERS WALK AWAY WITH AN UNCLEAR UNDERSTANDING.

SPEAK UP: WHAT TO SAY

Let's take a lesson from Donald Miller and go with this model of what to say.

First, here's an example he shared. Imagine you're at a dinner party, and Person One responds to the question "What do you do?" with this: "I'm a personal chef." Now, imagine Person Two says, "You know how at the end of a long day you come home and you don't know what to make for dinner? I help solve that problem as I'm a personal chef."

What a difference!

TO BE EFFECTIVE, YOU NEED TO START BY SHARING THE PROBLEM YOU SOLVE IN A WAY THAT'S RELATABLE TO YOUR AUDIENCE.

Here's the prompt for the "What I do" formula:

You know how (person and problem)? I help them to (solution). In my work, it would be something like, "You know how women often hold back from sharing their ideas? I work with them to overcome self-doubt and speak with confidence in both their presence and their message."

Part of the problem is narrowing it down. That's where we end up in a jumbled mess of words because we don't want to choose, or we simply can't find the most concise way to capture it. We also want to leave ourselves available to any and all clients who might choose us.

Most of the time, I see people sharing way too much. We dump data on people, and then they can't make heads or tails out of what it is that we've shared. You don't want to confuse people (see Chapter 5).

WHAT'S HOLDING YOU BACK?

One of the biggest issues with women I see is the hesitancy to self-promote. We're afraid of sounding arrogant or people thinking that we're bragging.

We *have* to get out of that mindset.

What does self-promotion mean anyway?

It's simply sharing who you are and what you do so the world knows you exist! I have a whole podcast episode on this: Episode 27: Three Tips to Promote Yourself with Ease.

Scan the QR code above for quick access

Here are two questions to ask yourself:

1. Why is it so hard for me? 80%+ is mindset, so tackle your fears and self-doubt first (go to Chapter 2 for specific exercises on how to combat those).

2. How does what I do serve the world? If we recognize that our gifts and talents help others, we may be more willing to share them.

Questions to help you:

- What I'm most proud of is...
- What that demonstrates about me is...
- My best quality is...
- Why that's helpful to others is...

Start there and see where that lands. You can also do what I recommend to my clients: ask five people you trust in different parts of your life what your top five positive qualities are. You'll notice themes and feel pretty darned good about yourself, too!

Another issue people have is in introducing themselves. I continue to marvel at the challenge this poses. We don't know what to say and usualy feel unprepared.

Always be ready with an introduction! Above all else, the one thing to prepare for is to talk about yourself. We're often asked to introduce ourselves. In business and in our personal lives.

Here's how:

Use my PPU introduction formula to be ready at a moment's notice.

- Personal: Say something personal (from Minnesota, now San Francisco, married with two kitties)
- Professional: Share your profession (professional speaker for high achieving corporate women over 40)
- Unique: Offer something unique about you (love following dreams—lived in Manhattan for my 50th birthday month)

Here's how it might sound in conversation:

Personal: "I'm originally from Minnesota and now live in San Francisco with my husband and two kitties after packing my bags in the mid-90s to follow a dream of living in SF.

Professional: Professionally, I'm a speaker supporting women in business to stand out with confidence in their presence and their message.

Unique: One unique thing about me is that I love adventure. An example of that is deciding to live in Manhattan for the whole month of October for my 50th birthday. I rented a place and spent 30 glorious days living like a local."

Try that out, and let me know how it goes! You'll be focused and memorable.

SPEAK FIRST

My client, Joni, a senior director in engineering from a Fortune 100 company, learned a valuable lesson. After being in the same job for several years, she was looking for a new internal opportunity. The manager of the department with a job opening made two eye-opening observations about Joni that were holding her back. The observations made it nearly impossible for the manager to determine if Joni was a potential candidate:

1. Joni didn't put on her camera in meetings, so the manager had no visual read of her.

2. She didn't speak up or contribute.

This was hard to hear but extremely helpful. She vocalized that she doesn't have a problem speaking up, but she doesn't feel the need to do it in most meetings as everyone else is talking; even speaking over each other sometimes. She didn't want to be a part of that.

Here's my advice: share something to show your opinion or perspective. Even if others have said something similar, add your name to the hat. People will have no way to see your brilliance if you don't say something.

Also, speak first. Jump in and contribute right away. This calms any nerves or at least puts them at bay. It prevents you from trying to figure out what to say later that adds value and isn't a repeat of what others have said.

WHEN YOU HOLD BACK BECAUSE YOU'RE UNSURE IF WHAT YOU HAVE TO SAY IS RELEVANT ENOUGH OR WILL BE APPRECIATED, YOU GIVE AWAY YOUR INFLUENCE AND LESSEN YOUR CHANCE FOR IMPACT.

With each person who speaks before you, you begin to compare their thoughts to yours and build a story that what they have to say is better than what you have to say. In that case, you likely won't end up speaking at all.

Be first! Even if others disagree, you have powerful opinions that need to be heard and you'll never know their impact if you leave them bottled up.

SUCCESS FROM SHOWING UP AND SPEAKING UP

How I accidentally started a podcast:

It was 8:50am, and I was in bed exhausted, having gone to sleep at 2am. I had committed to a virtual networking event that began at 9am. All I wanted was to go back to sleep.

"Get up. You said you were joining, and you need to show up." That's what I said to myself as I was lying there half-asleep ready to turn over again.

At the meeting, I met Ebony Wiley, who I felt an instant connection with. When we met the following week with the intent to get more acquainted, she asked if I had ever thought of having a podcast. My immediate thought was, "not really." Certainly not in the near future. She said she could help me launch it, and the following week we came up with a plan.

That was November of 2020. By January 2021, my Ignite Your Confidence podcast had launched. As I write this in April 2022, I've recorded and published over 60 episodes.

All because I showed up and said yes to the adventure!

UP WITH PEOPLE

Did you know that I've traveled all over the world performing in a leadership and educational program? All because I said yes to an invitation. I was a junior at Lafayette College, and my sorority sister had been a drummer in a group called Up with People.

She'd taken a year off college to do it, traveling on two continents and living with host families. One night when I was supposed to be at a sorority officers' meeting, my drummer sister "kidnapped" me so we could go to a performance of the troupe in Allentown, Pennsylvania.

I interviewed and got in. From the summer after college in 1990 through 1994, I toured with them, meeting hundreds of incredible people from all over the world.

All because I said yes to the invitation.

CLUBHOUSE

This social media app has rocked my world. In early 2021, I was on a women's entrepreneurial Facebook group, and someone was asking for speakers to join her "room" on Clubhouse. I had no idea what that meant or what Clubhouse was, but I was determined to find out. All I knew was that it required an invitation, and I was determined to get one.

I started asking around on social media, and within a couple of hours, I was in. That was January 9, 2021. Thank you to Tiffany Castagno, who gave me the invitation to join.

This is where I built my platform and grew to new levels of influence. I had no idea how much fun it would be and how empowered I would feel by being involved. My business grew exponentially, and every time I was on the app, I learned something about myself and was able to give back.

This is where I learned how valuable my skills are and how many women I can help. Confident communication is desperately needed, and most don't know the formula, so my toolbox was a welcome solution for people. I was thrilled to support, and I poured out to all that were there.

I could write a book on my experience with it (hey, I guess I am now!).

IT TAUGHT ME THE VALUE—AGAIN AND AGAIN —OF SHOWING UP AND SPEAKING UP.

That's how I reached a level of success there. It worked for me!

On a daily basis, showing up and speaking up led to incredible opportunities. Such as:

- Being on my first TV show, Brunch with Courtney Perna
- Being featured as the lead of the story in Inc Magazine for how to grow your business on Clubhouse (got a client at 2am from the bathtub while in Napa at a retreat after eating Tiramisu too late at night)
- An international speaking engagement

Remember to pay attention. You never know when an opportunity will strike.

7

ASK FOR WHAT YOU WANT: NEGOTIATE TO COLLABORATE

My love for negotiating began when I was six years old. Dad gave me a few dollars at the flea market and told me never to pay full price. A whole new world was opened to me when I learned that this is possible.

I put the money in my cherished Native American pouch and set out on the tar pavement with a seemingly endless supply of merchants displaying their wares. I loved seeing how low in price they would go. I was confident walking away if they didn't give it to me at the price I wanted.

It was exhilarating. I was confident and proud of my skills. Little did I know how beneficial that experience would be for my future.

I may not be a cute little kid anymore effortlessly wooing the merchants, but I've learned a few things since that have carried me throughout my adult life.

DAD'S WISDOM IMPARTED

My dad was known for saying, "The squeaky wheel gets the grease," and "you won't get, if you don't ask." He was relentless when it came to getting what he wanted. He was frugal, resourceful, and savvy. A child of the Great Depression, he worked hard to provide for nine kids.

I took his words to heart. I saw the results of asking. He used to tell me, "With enough persistence and determination, you can get whatever you want." He modeled grit.

I like to think I embody those characteristics, too. I'm tenacious. I expect that I'm going to get whatever I go after. I set my sights on something and work hard to make it happen, rallying the people and resources needed to get to the goal.

How about you? What's something you want to ask for but have been holding out?

I've never had a problem asking. I'm always of the philosophy that the worst that can happen is a "no." And then you move on to the next person. I did well selling Mary Kay, and one of the things I learned at 18 years old is to expect 50 "no's" to get to a "yes" for a sale.

That's what I learned and believed to be true. Because I didn't expect it to come easy, I didn't have a problem with rejection. Expectations setting is important. You have to have an idea of what reality is.

Fast forward to 2020, when I was building my email list.

AT FIRST, IT WAS HARD WHEN SOMEONE UNSUBSCRIBED BECAUSE IT FELT SO PERSONAL, BUT EVENTUALLY, I STARTED CELEBRATING WHEN THAT HAPPENED. THAT MEANT I WAS ELIMINATING THOSE THAT DIDN'T FIT MY TARGET AUDIENCE, AND I WAS GETTING CLOSER TO THOSE THAT DID.

BE CREATIVE WITH YOUR ASK

In 2000 when I negotiated the salary for my first big corporate position overseeing Human Resources, I was quite proud of myself. I thought long, hard, and creatively about what to ask. Besides securing a higher salary than I could've ever expected, I negotiated a better title, a signing bonus, and more vacation time. It was one of my biggest and early wins professionally.

If you're negotiating for a job, think about what's important to you besides salary. It might be:

Title
Flex schedule
More vacation
Work remotely
Promotion within X period of time

Exposure to the executive team
Signing bonus

And some phrases that work well:

- "Can we get closer to ...?"
- "I was looking for the high end of the range..."
- "What else besides salary would you be able to offer?"

You have to think about what matters most to you and what's a win for the other party, too.

Sometimes it's a matter of discovery. I recall in Stephen Covey's *The 7 Habits of Highly Effective People,* there was a story about someone in an office setting who wanted the window open, and the other person wanted it shut.

When they actually talked to each other rather than digging their heels into their respective positions, they found out something important that changed the game. Person One wanted fresh air, and Person Two didn't like drafts blowing on him. Their solution was brilliantly simple: open a window in the other room so there would be fresh air without a draft!

Open dialogue is so important.

BE IRRESISTIBLE

In 2006 I interviewed for a job that ended up being the job of my dreams for 14 years.

In 1999, I visualized and wrote down what I wanted my dream job to be: Corporate trainer traveling around the world working 2-3 days a week. In 2006 I landed that job. Almost exactly as I had imagined it, but better.

Here's how it happened. Remember the seize opportunities chapter? We have to pay attention but also be irresistible when we show up.

- The leader of a women's networking group that I was in was asked to speak at the annual President Hoover prayer breakfast at the Westin San Francisco. She didn't want to do it, so she told the organizers: "I know someone who would!"
- I spoke to an audience of 200 people that day and met Mrs. S. She approached me and asked if I'd like to be part of a conference she was organizing. I said, "yes."
- During one of her meetings at her home, I met her husband, who owned a communications company. He heard I was facilitating at Gap Inc and said, "Can you send me your resume tomorrow?"
- And just like that, I had an interview with my future boss.
- At the interview, I presented something

unexpected: my celebration portfolio. It was a collection of thank you notes and testimonials from my work.

- The path was laid out before me. All I needed to do was show up!
- The bonus? I negotiated more than expected and went on to create two different roles there that I proactively initiated over the years.

BESIDES PAYING ATTENTION AND SHOWING UP, YOU NEED TO KNOW YOUR WORTH AND COMMUNICATE YOUR VALUE.

KNOW YOUR WORTH

Too often, women downplay their strengths. We've got to stop this! We minimize ourselves and even get physically smaller.

More on this In Chapter 10, when we talk about what to say and what not to say (hint: stop saying "I've just got a little tip for you" and say, "I've got a tip for you").

Imagine you're saying the prior sentence. Sometimes we hunch our shoulders in or tilt our heads to the side as if we aren't worthy of sharing something or being in the room.

Sit up and stand tall.

You've got to recognize that you are worthy simply by existing. Simultaneously, when it comes to a job or a business deal, the fact remains that we have to show our worth.

> *YOU CAN'T WAIT FOR SOMEONE TO NOTICE YOU'RE DOING A GOOD JOB AND HOPE THAT THEY'LL SEE YOU AND SAY SOMETHING.*

ONE OF MY BIGGEST MISTAKES

In one of my corporate jobs, we were incorporating a more formal leadership team, and my boss, the company president, asked me to be a part of it. I was thrilled! Recognizing that most people on the team were director level or above (and I wasn't—technically I was a senior manager), I asked what my title might change to (my first problem: passive question!).

My boss was distracted when I asked, and she said we'd have to figure that out. I passively implied, "Well, everyone else is a director or above, so..." thinking that was an ask. My first mistake!

I knew better, but I truly wasn't conscious of my mistake and the magnitude of how this would affect me. A few months later, and after I was already on the leadership team, I brought it up to another decision maker in the company. The discussion didn't go anywhere (second mistake—I would've asked for a title change or promotion plan by the time the leadership team was in place—if I had a do-over).

Fast forward eight months to my review over a delicious lunch in the financial district of San Francisco. I was expecting a promotion to Director. It didn't happen. Sue sensed I was disappointed and asked me what was wrong. That's when I shared my expectation, and she didn't remember the initial conversation. I was surprised at first, but upon reflection, I realized I was the problem. I didn't make a direct ask.

In hindsight, here's what I would've done differently: I would've said I wanted to be promoted to director and asked what it would take to get there: where I needed to improve and by when. I would've asked for mentoring and proposed a draft timeline.

Here's my own psychoanalysis that may help you, too.

Why didn't I ask in the first place? I'm normally confident. This time I felt really vulnerable. The leadership team role was ambiguous. Somehow, I felt exposed and unsure. Did I really deserve a seat at the table? I'm so honored to be a part of it; I better not ask for anything else. Maybe if I hope enough, she'll notice and promote me without me having to ask.

Yikes! Even I (who teaches this stuff)! Many problems with my mindset at the time, but the one that stands out most is not knowing my worth. I was a valuable member of the team, and still, I didn't recognize it to the full extent.

This may be you, too. Dive into what the root cause of that might be. It's worth exploring, and hopefully, you can save yourself from making the same mistake I did.

MY BEST NEGOTIATION SUCCESS STORY

My favorite negotiation success story happened right before the Pandemic. In March of 2020, I secured a lucrative coaching contract and was tickled pink.

Once Covid hit, the company changed its mind. Months of gentle follow-up led to nothing. I had almost given up when a year and a half later, they resurfaced. They were ready for me to coach their manager. When I looked back at the original contract, I realized two things: 1) I would charge a higher amount now, and 2) I would propose a longer timeframe.

I went back to them and shared that what I continue to learn in my coaching work is that it takes time, intention, and support for clients to make sustainable changes. I shared that I'm in more demand now, so that my rate is higher, and I proposed a six-month contract.

> *I QUOTED NEARLY THREE TIMES AS MUCH AS I HAD ORIGINALLY, AND THEY SAID YES! I WAS OVER THE MOON—BEST ACCOMPLISHMENT YET IN MY NEGOTIATION LIFE.*

Here's what's key: I asked. You have to ask to play the game! Otherwise, you'll never know.

What happens if they say "no"? Which is an important possibility to be ready to tackle.

Follow the best advice from Alex Carter (Clinical Professor of Law at Columbia Law School and WSJ bestselling author of *Ask for More*): Ask, "What concerns do you have?" That is the best way to turn a "no" into a "yes." Most people are afraid of rejection, so they don't.

Or it doesn't even occur to them. This will unveil reasons they may never have mentioned if you didn't bother to ask. You may be surprised. You likely can rectify their concerns and readjust. You never know!

COMMUNICATING YOUR VALUE

One of my longtime friends is a real estate agent who lost out on a sale because the client decided to go with another agent.

Her mentor said something powerful: "The other agent was better at selling discount than you were at communicating value." Boom! How's that for hitting you across the head?!

WE'VE GOT TO FOCUS ON WHAT VALUE WE BRING TO THE TABLE AND COMMUNICATE THAT WITH CLARITY.

Figuring out what the other party cares about is a good start to even see if you're the right person—with whatever it may be: a promotion, new business, or something else.

Another friend of mine says, "Karen, we're Gucci. No discounts!" The key is to stand your ground with yourself and not waver; recognize what you do and don't offer.

One of the best decisions I made in 2003 when I first left corporate to start my business, was deciding that I would never "need" clients. What I meant by that was to never be desperate for clients such that I would work with anyone. I wanted to be selective.

Granted, at first, I pretty much did work with anyone who wanted to work with me (gotta start somewhere!), but my turning point was when I said my rates without wavering. When I stopped saying I could work with whatever budget they had. When I stopped doing that and stood by my rates, my clients increased.

Funny how that is.

Communicating your value so that it's crystal clear isn't always easy, especially when there's a lot at stake. Do your best to first identify what matters to you and where you will or won't compromise. Be flexible and also clear. Be willing to walk away whenever possible. People can smell desperate.

Like the Challenger Sales approach (Dixon and Adamson), you need to be able to educate potential clients or hiring managers. When people question my rates, sometimes all that's needed is a little education. For example, once I explain that they're paying for expertise that I've established over nearly three decades, that changes their perspective.

Another example came from an acquaintance who emcee's events. She shared that a potential client asked if her hourly rate was around $200. It was closer to $10K, so there was a huge gap. She kindly shared with him that you're not just getting her time. You're getting her voice, her experience, and her ability to energize the room and handle anything such as conflict or tech difficulties; to give the best experience possible. He was embarrassed and didn't mean to "insult." He simply didn't know.

It's *our* job to communicate our value. No one else is going to do that for us.

BRING THEM INTO A BIGGER PURPOSE

When I was securing speakers for my 2020 women's summit, Ignite Your Confidence, I learned a powerful lesson from Alex Carter.

BRING YOUR AUDIENCE INTO A PURPOSE BIGGER THAN THEMSELVES.

Instead of asking people to speak at my event (which is also more self-serving), I started asking, "Want to be part of a movement empowering women?"

That also made me feel good to share with them. We all want to make a difference bigger than ourselves. It worked!

Other examples could be:

Instead of saying, "Will you donate blood at the blood drive," say, "Want to be part of saving someone's life?"

Or instead of "I'd like a promotion," say "I'd like to expand the reach of our marketing department."

Similar to what was shared in Chapter 5, we have to know our audience and gear our message to them if we want to influence (and have a better chance of getting what we want).

DIRECT VS. PASSIVE ASKS

We have to recognize when we're passively asking something so we can adjust and therefore get a more desirable result. A passive ask sounds like this:

- "If you're interested, let me know."
- "If you think this is something you'd like to do, I'm happy to talk more about it."
- "Perhaps you'd like to..."

Instead of that route, be direct and say this instead:

- "Are you interested?"
- "Is this something you'd like to do?"
- "Would you like to?"

We're socially conditioned to go with the passive ask because most of us fear rejection. We want to have an out, so we don't have to hear "no."

GOING WITH THE HARDER OPTION OF ASKING DIRECTLY TAKES COURAGE BUT WILL MAKE YOU MUCH MORE EFFECTIVE IN YOUR COMMUNICATION AS A LEADER.

And get you closer to what you want even quicker!

FOLLOW UP

Most of us do 2-3 follow-up emails, and then we give up if we haven't heard back. We make up a story that they're not interested in us or what we have to offer. While this may be true, there are so many other possibilities of why they didn't respond.

More importantly, I find that the gentle persistence technique works best. Most people are either really busy, or they don't want to say no, so they don't say anything. You also have to determine how important the connection is.

THE 3D'S

In 2019 I put a stake in the ground to become a professional speaker on my own. I had been doing that for years for a wonderful company, but I knew it was time to leave and blaze my own trail.

Have you ever felt stuck?

For two years, I knew there was more for me, but I couldn't figure out what it was.

I WAS STUCK WITH NO IDEA HOW TO GET OUT. I FELT LIKE A RACEHORSE LOCKED BEHIND THE GATES. I HAD SO MUCH ENERGY TO FOCUS ON SOMETHING MEANINGFUL, BUT I COULDN'T DETERMINE WHAT.

It finally hit me.

Have you ever held a dream back due to some fear? Maybe fear of failure or even success? I had to face myself and acknowledge that it was time—my dream since I was a kid needed to be realized. I want to speak on stadium-sized stages empowering women to be free! I want to support them with tools to be confident communicators.

When I saw Jess Ekstrom's Instagram ad for Mic Drop Workshop, I was hooked. At first, I thought, who is this person with headphones walking through an airport? She doesn't look very professional!

Look at me now—a raging fan. After watching the ad a few times and then seeing her webinar, I wanted *in*. She was so relatable and real. And she had a level of success that I could see for myself.

I waited until the final hour. At 11:59pm in my Nashville Marriott hotel, I paid $1000 to join her program. It was a leap of faith. It was expensive, and I had no real idea if it would help me. But the rest is history. The community alone of like-minded women with the dream of becoming keynote speakers has been worth it.

Looking back, a formula ensued that can help you, too: The 3D's. My dear friend, Jeanne Grabowski (Career Transition and Brand Strategist), brought this one to light.

The first D is to Decide what you want. I decided I would embrace my dream of being a professional speaker. Remember the scene in *The Notebook* where Ryan Gosling's character says, "What do you want?!" One of my favorite movie moments. Deciding can be hard.

The second D is to Declare it. Tell everyone you know and ask for referrals or support. People are natural problem solvers. Ask them to help you solve your problem. Be specific in what you're asking.

BE SPECIFIC

One of the biggest beefs I had as an HR manager was when people would send me resumes saying, "whatever job you have that you think I can do, let me know." It drove me nuts. I don't care what your background is. What do you *want* to be doing? What role are you shooting for? Don't put that on me. Tell me what you want.

Technically, you're giving away your power when you do that. Plus, you make it really hard on the HR person (or your friend, family member, or mentor) who wants to help you, but you're not telling them how, which is your responsibility.

The third D is to Do it. Go after it. Take action. Make it happen.

That's what I did, and it worked. How about you? Where could you employ the 3D's?

MORE TIPS ON HOW TO ASK

- Prompts for your lead into the conversation: "What I'd like to get from this is..." or "What I'd like to talk about is..."
- Focus on adding value: "What I'd like to offer you is..." or "Where I believe I could add value is..."
- Share your story in a way that's relevant to your audience: "My background ties in beautifully to your mission" or "In doing research about your organization, I found that you... and I connected to that because..."
- Be passionate: Show it in your voice and facial expression
- Avoid getting attached to the outcome: You don't want to come across as desperate. Try: "Don't believe me, believe what my clients say..."

8

BOUNDARIES: THE POWER OF SAYING "NO"

Setting boundaries didn't come easily for me. Growing up in Minnesota and being my mom's daughter—it was all about accommodating everyone else. You moved mountains to do what other people wanted. It was modeled as the right thing to do. It truly didn't feel like I had a choice. I didn't know anything else.

Fast forward to adulthood, when I was learning the value of boundaries and working hard to establish them instead of saying yes to everyone: I had left corporate to start my business in coaching and was at a crossroads. How do I say "no" to friends who wanted my career guidance when they were used to me doing it for free?

Sitting in my therapist's office in the Financial District of San Francisco on her comfy brown leather couch, I was confronted with what felt like a scary but necessary choice. I needed to say "no" to my friend, Katy, who had asked me to review/edit her resume. I left my session that day equipped with what to say. I proudly returned the following week with a report back that I did it!

Here's what I said: "Katy, I'd love to help. Now that I've left my corporate job, this is what I do for a living. If you'd like to pay me, I charge $X/hour. Does that work for you?" Whew! That was scary to say, but it felt so good to stand my ground!

As expected, she didn't want to pay, but what felt good was offering her another option: sending her my resume as a template. It cost me nothing. She took me up on that!

Since that conversation, I've become increasingly better with boundaries to where they're rarely an issue for me anymore.

What about you? What's a boundary that you need to set that you've been putting off?

WHAT DO YOU NEED TO SAY "NO" TO SO YOU CAN SAY "YES" TO SOMETHING ELSE?

Remember:

"No" is a complete sentence. :) The Minnesota Nice in me suggests you could throw in a "no, thank you" to that sentence.

YOU GET TO DECIDE

I was facilitating a corporate training where the women were giving feedback to each other. One woman turned to another and said, "How do you spell your name? Is it Christy or Kristy?" Christy said, "It doesn't matter. Whatever you prefer."

What?! I turned to Christy and said, "Of course it matters! It's your name!" We had an entire sidebar discussion on this. It's about who you are; your identity. You're giving your power away when you let the other person decide.

Only *you* get to decide who you are. When someone asks you how to spell or pronounce your name, they want to get it right out of respect for you. When you reject that, it puts the other person in an awkward position and leaves them hanging. It also can make you come across as undefined.

UNDEFINED PEOPLE CAN BE CONFUSING AND UNCLEAR. DEFINED PEOPLE ARE CLEAR AND CONFIDENT.

They know who they are, and that makes others feel more secure and comfortable. What you see is what you get. You're not left wondering.

YOUR PERSONAL LEADERSHIP BRAND

Who do you want to be in the world? This is a powerful and big question to ponder. How do you want people to talk about you when they leave your presence?

It's important to start with a foundation, so you're clear on who you want to be and how you're representing that identity. My mom's motto was to "Be Kind." That's how she showed up in the world. Always. She had one of the most consistent brands I know.

Give yourself grace as you reflect on the question of who you want to be. Start with a list of values as a starting point. If you had to boil it down to 3-5 things that you value most in the world, what would those be?

My top value is connection, closely followed by celebration and communication. That shapes much of what I do. Ask people around you that are close to you: "What do I represent to you?" "How do I stand out?" "What makes me different from everyone else?"

You can think of it as a research study. Once you get some input, see what resonates for you, and then write those things down.

Circa 2007, I was in a random hotel room on a business trip praying for God to give me a Bible verse that most represents me. I had heard of people praying for that, and I remember thinking, "God, I want a life verse!" Within moments after opening my Bible, I was looking at Hebrews

10:24: "Encourage one another to outbursts of love and good deeds."

It immediately struck me at my core. Yes! That's it! It also happens to be my birthday (October 24). God is good.

First of all, I love the word "burst" which is how I feel a lot. I'm bursting with joy or some new idea on the regular. If all I did was encourage people and make them feel important, I'd consider myself a success in this life.

WHEN PEOPLE ARE AROUND ME, I WANT THEM TO FEEL SEEN, HEARD AND ACCEPTED FOR EXACTLY WHO THEY ARE.

It may not be a Bible verse for you, but perhaps it's a word or a phrase that best represents you. My mom's guiding value was to be kind, and that's how she lived her life. It's a way to ground yourself and also help others get to know who you are. It also doesn't mean you have to tell anyone. It can be just for you.

It's very helpful, though, when making decisions. For example, when Chris and I got married, I asked him what he wanted our home life to represent. "Peaceful, safe, and fun." and it stuck. Anytime we have to make a decision, particularly a challenging one, we decide through that lens.

We had a huge conflict with a neighbor once, and after weeks of strife, Chris reminded me, "Is this who we want to be? Is it representing our value of peace?" That was a hard "no," so we dropped it (even though it pains me because we were so wronged!).

IT WAS TIME TO LET IT GO AND BE FREE. FORGIVENESS IS ABOUT FREEING YOURSELF.

Another way to get clear on your brand is to write your eulogy. What would you want people to say about you when you're gone? Then ask yourself if you're living the way you want to live that represents who you want to be.

We can't leave this section without mentioning your purpose. What's your "why?" as Simon Sinek says (author of *Start with Why*). When you know why you're doing something, your actions and decisions are much clearer. You know who you are and what you stand for.

When I decided that my mission was to reach 10 million women to overcome self-doubt and speak with confidence, everything became clearer. When you have a purpose and a goal to reach, you know what to say "yes" to and what to say "no" to.

THE POWER OF CHOICE

There was a time when I worked with several lawyers as clients related to a career change. The theme was enlightening. Many of them had chosen their careers due to their parents or grandparents; someone influential in their lives who convinced them to do it. Yet, most of them were unhappy. That's why they were working with me—to make that change.

I implore you to remember: you always have a choice. For so much of my life, I didn't think I did. Employ the power of self-agency.

When Chris (my husband) and I were dating (or rather, on a break from dating!) I was seeing a therapist who was guiding me in the relationship. At one point, he said, "What do you want [related to being or not being with Chris]? I said, "I don't know what Chris wants yet."

WHAT?!

My therapist said, "But, what do *you* want?"

Boom. That was the first time I realized I had a choice.

I grew up with my dad making all of the decisions, and it was his way or the highway. I never thought of it being a choice I could make and own.

Owning your feelings and choices is hard. Once I realized, "Oh my gosh, I *do* want Chris!" then I had to face the possibility that he may not want me back. That felt scary.

Yet, freeing. Free yourself. I spent too much time thinking I had to do or be for someone else. Or that I needed permission.

Decide for yourself what you want. You have that power, and no one can take it away from you. Claim and take your seat!

You are more powerful than you think.

What are you choosing? Is there something in your life that you're choosing because someone else wanted that for you?

Decide today to choose for yourself. If you're worried about disappointing someone, remember: at the end of the day, it's your life.

"Between stimulus and response, there is a space.
In that space is our power to choose our response.
In our response lies our growth and our freedom."
-Victor Frankl

9

GRACE UNDER PRESSURE: THINKING ON YOUR FEET

A t a marriage retreat in Santa Rosa, CA, I learned a powerful concept that has become foundational for me in business. When faced with conflict or situations when you're not sure what action to take, use this formula. It works every time (thanks, Doug and Val Richardson).

It's simply this:

1. What's needed here?

2. What's required of me?

Ask yourself these two questions when faced with a situation you're not sure how to handle. This can take a nanosecond of time and help you regroup to prepare for what comes out of your mouth (or not) next.

It all comes back to knowing your audience. Pausing to think about what to do is a great technique to stay composed and focused (though often easier said than done).

As human beings, we are wired to solve problems.

Our knee-jerk reaction is to talk.

To solve.

To give advice.

Don't do that.

At least not right away.

Often the best response is to stop, pause and breathe. This actually became the mantra of my client, the executive director of a non-profit organization who had a tendency to react instead of responding in board meetings. This made her come across as the opposite of composed and wasn't boding well for her position.

She committed to saying to herself, "stop, pause, breathe," when she wanted to make a comment. It helped her to slow down and be composed before she spoke.

When emotions are high, it's easier to react instead of to respond. Do whatever you can to prevent that.

What technique works best for you?

Remember, how you respond is what people will judge. Not the behavior of the other person or people in the room. You want to put forth your best self in all situations.

Like all of our communications, thinking on your feet has two critical components: both what you say and how you say it.

WISH I HAD SAID THAT

Have you ever been stuck with what to say in the moment, and then when it's too late, you think of the *perfect* response?! I know I have. It's so hard when you're thrown off guard. These tips will help you compose and calm yourself. The punchline is that it's really about breathing and pausing! And trusting yourself.

MENTAL AGILITY

We need to be flexible when it comes to thinking on our feet. Be ready for anything and prepare yourself for the unexpected. You may need to pivot or switch up what you had planned.

BE ATTUNED TO WHAT YOUR AUDIENCE NEEDS SO YOU CAN SERVE THEM IN THE BEST POSSIBLE WAY.

One of the most effective ways to practice mental agility is to take an improv course. It will help you focus on what matters most in the moment.

Stay Present.

This can be hard when you're nervous or unsure. Maybe your confidence is shaken, and you're not clear about what to do. If you've got notes or are in the middle of a presentation and you're thrown off by something, stay present with what's happening in the room.

You'll be much more effective if you focus on connection versus what you prepared, although I recognize you want to still look smart and credible. Trust that you know more than you think.

Stay strong in your presence and message: You've got this. Be confident in who you are and what you know.

Acknowledge. Show empathy. Be kind and direct.

For example, someone asks you a tough question:

Pause first to compose yourself.

Acknowledge their question and empathize, if appropriate.

"You're absolutely right, many people do disagree with this," or "That's a valid concern," or "I can understand why you feel that way."

Repeat the point of your message to stay focused and on track.

"Let's get back to..."

Stop. Pause. Breathe.

If you don't know the answer, say you don't know, but you'll get back to them. And, make sure you follow up!

HOW TO HANDLE INTERRUPTIONS

You're on a roll, and then someone breaks your train of thought by interrupting. It can be so frustrating. See my top tips below for what to do.

- Your presence: Be mindful of your body language and voice. Display confidence: shoulders back, lean forward, and speak with conviction over hesitation. Look into the camera (if virtual) or directly at people, so they feel a connection to you.
- Your words: Use an acknowledgement bridge which is simply a way to acknowledge what they said and then move the point forward. Such as "Those are great ideas! Give me a moment to finish, and I'll turn it back over to the room." Or, "Thank you for sharing your opinion. Hold on for a minute, and I'll complete my thought." "Bob, I love your ideas, and I have one that I'd like to share as well, which is...."
- With chronic interrupters, speak to them privately and/or create a "no interrupting" ground rule at your meetings. Proactively stating the meeting parameters up front makes it a lot easier to address any issues later.
- Be willing to look at yourself.

If you don't come across as strong and confident (while being approachable and inviting) when you start talking, people will not trust that you're leading with authority and will be more inclined to interrupt you.

- Speak with conviction and not hesitation. Project your voice.

HOW TO INTERRUPT

If *you* want to interrupt, say "I'd like to interject," or "Here's what I'll add to that thought," or "Excuse me (only if needed), I want to add to that" along with the prior tips on presence and the acknowledgement bridge.

Make sure you come across with strength in your voice and in your posture when you interrupt. Be kind yet assertive. You don't need to ask for permission, such as, "Could I add something please?" or "Is it okay if I say something?" Too many women do that, and we've got to stop.

> ***WHEN YOU WANT TO SHARE YOUR OPINION OR YOUR IDEA, AND YOU'RE LOOKING FOR A WAY TO DO IT DIPLOMATICALLY, YOU CAN JUMP IN WITH, "HERE'S MY VOTE, OR HERE'S MY OPINION."***

That's what worked for me when I was getting more comfortable sharing my ideas. Before that, my boss surprised me by saying, "You always ask everyone else what they think. I want to know what *you* think." That's when I realized I needed to change that. It became a lot easier for me to share my opinion when I started using the term "Here's my vote."

INTENTION VS. IMPACT

Have you ever been misunderstood? You may have said or done something that came across differently than you meant it to.

For example, when I was managing a team, one of my new employees did an incredible job facilitating for a client, going above and beyond. I was so excited to recognize him in front of our team and made a big deal about it at one of our quarterly meetings. Much to my surprise, he told me that he had felt put on the spot, and it made him uncomfortable. Wow. I would've never known if he hadn't told me. I'm so grateful he gave me the chance to apologize.

That was a huge lesson for me in intention vs. impact. Also, always ask how your employees like to be recognized.

Here's another example: I got an email once that felt very transactional, and I'm sure the sender's intention was different from her impact. It surprised me because it was in response to someone who had referred me to this therapist and was highly regarded, so I expected a friendlier email. Instead of "Wonderful! I have so much respect for Betty. Here's my availability." She launched immediately into the transaction (her availability) with no pleasantries or acknowledgement of the referral.

The result? It made me significantly less inclined to consider her as a therapist. I didn't email her back for days. It was only because of my friend's recommendation that I pursued it.

Sometimes we won't even know that we did something that had an unintended impact.

Has this ever happened to you?

LEAN INTO CHALLENGING CONVERSATIONS

Besides the two framing questions where we started this chapter, here's how to lean into challenging conversations:

- Seek first to understand their perspective. You can start by asking a question (e.g., "please share how this landed with you; please tell me your viewpoint; I'd like to hear what you think").

- Be open to hearing what they have to say, then pause and stop talking to let them speak after you ask.
- Be ready to hear something unexpected (we're generally quick to make assumptions, and you might be surprised at what you hear that offers insight and clarity).
- Consider my ASS ;) formula: Ask (a question), Seek (to understand), and then Share (only after you've heard them speak, then you can share how it felt or landed for you).
- Share the impact their behavior had - remember it's not a personal attack. It's how they came across. "Came across" are the magic words; i.e., instead of "you're such a jerk," which defines the person as a fixed state; use "you came across as a jerk in that moment" to show it was just in that moment. We can all be jerks at times!
- Agree on the next steps. What is your request after this? What are you asking of the person?

WHAT THAT SOUNDS LIKE

Let's use an example on the interruptions theme. Pretend Colleen interrupts you regularly in meetings, but you've never talked with her about it.

Here's what you could say:

You: "Hey, Colleen. Got a minute?"

Colleen: "Sure. What's up?"

You: "I've noticed something in our meetings that's become a theme, and I wanted to check in with you about it. Sometimes when I'm speaking, you interject. Are you aware of that?"

Colleen: "Not at all! It hadn't even occurred to me. I can get passionate about things for sure."

You: "Ah, that makes sense. It's hard for me when anyone interrupts me because I lose my train of thought, and then I get thrown off."

Colleen: "Had no idea I did it, though. That definitely wasn't my intent!"

You: "I understand. Thanks for hearing me. If you could be more conscious of it in the future, I'd greatly appreciate it."

Colleen: "Absolutely! My apologies. I'll be mindful of it next time."

I recognize that is an ideal scenario, and it usually doesn't go that smoothly.

Let's say Colleen gets defensive and says, "No I don't [interrupt]" or "I'm just passionate. It's no big deal."

You could say, "Ah. It sounds like we are having two different experiences. I wanted to be really intentional and bring this up only if it became a theme. I respect your perspective, and I'd like to share mine. Is that okay with you?"

Colleen: "I guess. Sure."

You: "When I'm talking, I lose my train of thought when interruptions happen. I'm easily distracted and lose focus. I realize you're saying you don't interrupt/you're just passionate. I'd like to ask if you could be mindful of that in the future. Just in case you might be tempted to interject."

Colleen: "Ok. I still don't think I've interrupted you, but ok."

You: "I appreciate you hearing me. It means a lot."

GETTING PAST MISTAKES WHEN PRESENTING

When I first started out, I remember advancing to the wrong slide, and I would say, "Oops!" making it obvious. Now, when I do that, I quickly move to the correct slide.

IF YOU'RE PRESENTING AND YOU MAKE A MISTAKE, DON'T CALL ATTENTION TO IT. THE AUDIENCE ONLY GETS WHAT YOU GIVE THEM, SO THEY DON'T KNOW IF YOU MESSED UP.

Unless it was super obvious, keep it to yourself and move on. If it was a legit mistake, say "excuse me" and continue from there.

When you're presenting, remember that you control the experience. Generally speaking, people will follow you where you tell them to go. If it seems like you messed up, that's what they will think (if you show it). Otherwise, you'll stay clear of those distractions.

HOSTILE AUDIENCE MEMBER OR HECKLER

First, let's define the difference between hostile and difficult audience members.

Hostile is when the person has their own agenda, and you'll never win them over no matter how hard you try. It's futile.

A difficult audience member is just extremely curious or inquisitive.

Both can be challenging. With a hostile person, what often happens is that we end up trying to win them over at the expense of everyone else. Be careful to acknowledge them within reason.

With both, you can use the acknowledgement bridge plus a very important technique: maintain eye contact with others in the audience as much as the challenging people. You're responsible to the whole room, not just the one challenger.

Default phrases: "We can talk about this offline; let's put that on the parking lot and come back to it another time; for the sake of time, I'll need to move on."

HOW DO YOU DEAL WITH A MANSPLAINER OR A HE-PEATER?

If someone is mansplaining or shesplaining, it means that they are explaining something to you that's obvious or that you already know, usually in a patronizing way. You could say:

- "Got it, thanks. I'm aware of that."
- "Thanks. No need to explain. I'm aware."
- "You may not know it, but I'm an expert on this topic, too. I'm good. How about we talk about something else?"
- "You may not know it, but I'm versed on this topic, so no need to explain it to me."

It's tricky as you probably want to preserve the relationship, or at minimum, you don't want to come across as insulting. Most of the time, people aren't even aware they're doing it. If you want to inquire, you could ask questions of them to deflect the condescension. Last option that's always there for you? Walk away.

With he-peating or she-peating (when another person repeats what you've said and often takes your idea as their own), you could say, "Thanks for agreeing with what I said earlier. I'm glad you like my idea [that I said earlier]." "Oh, I already mentioned that. Thanks for reinforcing it!"

GIVING (AND GETTING) CONSTRUCTIVE FEEDBACK

When you hear the word "feedback," what do you feel? If I were to say, "I've got some feedback for you," you'd probably brace yourself for the negative.

As a word, "feedback" is neutral. Yet, as a society, it has connotations now, and most people steer clear of asking for it and of giving it.

FEEDBACK DOESN'T HAVE TO BE HARD OR UNCOMFORTABLE. ASK FOR IT REGULARLY, ESPECIALLY AS A LEADER. IT'S A RARE PERSON WHO SEEKS IT OUT, AND YOU WILL BE NOTICED AND APPRECIATED WHEN YOU DO THIS.

It shows humility and openness.

When giving feedback, a word replacement I like is "input." If you use that instead, the person may receive it more openly.

When you get feedback, pause and listen. Take it in. Don't get defensive. Do everything in your power to be calm. Inquire for more information with "Tell me more" or "Help me understand." You can be ready with an apology, if appropriate: "I'm sorry. That wasn't my intention. How can I do better next time?" or "What can I do?"

Out of each scenario above, think about the one that's most challenging for you. Commit to practicing one tip in the next week, and let me know how it goes!

10

WHAT TO SAY: SENTENCE PROMPTS FOR ANY INTERACTION

Sometimes all you want to know is what to say for an effective outcome. You need a recipe or a menu of options of the actual words.

This chapter addresses several scenarios and what to say for each. You'll get sentence prompts, formulas, and power questions all in one place.

FOCUS YOUR CONVERSATIONS

When someone says, "Tell me about yourself?" instead of launching into your life history, say, "What would you most like to know about me?"

That will keep it focused.

I learned the power of this strategy when I followed my own advice last year (yay, it worked!).

I was at the beginning of a call that I thought was for networking purposes only. When the other person asked me to tell her about myself, I was about to launch into my personal and professional history.

Instead, I paused and said, "What about me most interests you? She went on to talk about herself, and then she came around to this: "I guess what I most want to know is how you can help me."

At that moment, she became a client. I never would've seen that coming. I'm glad I stopped and focused the conversation. Whew!

Other ways to be focused and efficient in your communication:

- What I most want from this call is...
- How can I best support you (always a crowd-pleaser—surprises most people)?
- What I need is...
- How does that land for you?
- What do you think?
- Are you comfortable with that?
- How does that sound?
- Let's explore that further...
- Do you want my opinion, or do you just want me to listen?
- Here's what I don't want/need (use only with people you know well)

- In an effort to be as focused as possible, here's what I'm looking for in this conversation.
- Excuse me for interrupting. Here's how you can best help me...

When a conversation or meeting is going off the rails, say: "Let's get back to..."

SAY THIS, NOT THAT

When You Want to Ask "Why?!"

Instead of saying: "Why did you do that?" say: "What was your logic behind that?" or "Help me understand your reasoning behind that."

This is one of my favorite shifts in communication; especially when we're frustrated with someone and our go-to reaction is "why" (or maybe "why the heck?!"). Asking "what was your logic" comes across as much more inviting and shows an earnestness to understand. Along with that, it diffuses any potential frustration on the other person's part.

Another option is to frontload a conversation with "In an effort to understand," or "My intent is to understand. Can you clarify..." This takes them off of feeling potentially judged and refocuses them on the reasoning.

When You Disagree

When you disagree, instead of saying "I disagree with that," which puts people on the defensive almost immediately, say "I have another perspective."

---

or "I'd like to share another perspective." This feels more collaborative and expansive rather than feeling like you're on a different side or against them. It opens up possibilities and more creative discussion.

Avoid the Drop Down Menu

In one of my corporate jobs, I was often the subject matter expert on sales calls. I observed this a lot: after asking an open-ended question to potential clients, such as "What is your biggest communication challenge right now?" the sales people would quickly interrupt with a dropdown menu of options, such as "Is it with your team? Is it on the operations side? Is it conflict? Presence?"

Pause and let people respond with their own answer. When we give people options, usually none of those options are even correct. If we stay quiet and listen for their answer, it's a lot more efficient.

. . .

When You Need to Apologize

When you've wronged someone, say, "What can I do to make this right?" On top of "I'm sorry," say, "Will you forgive me?" It's a vulnerable question as you don't know what the answer will be, but it's powerful as it shows humility. It's also about the other person, not you. It puts the ball in their court.

When You Need To Overcome Hardship

When you're in a time of hardship, it can be tempting to ask, "Why me?" Instead, ask yourself, "How am I powerful?" This feeling of "why me?" goes hand in hand with a feeling of helplessness or powerlessness. You are fully self-sufficient, and you were given the strength needed to pass through all trials!

When You Need an Open Dialogue

> *INSTEAD OF, "DO YOU HAVE ANY QUESTIONS?" SAY, "WHAT QUESTIONS DO YOU HAVE?"*

The first one is a closed-ended question and can shut down

the conversation. The other assumes that the audience has questions and that you want to answer them. It provides a more open experience, and people will be more likely to ask.

When You Want a Better Relationship

In times of conflict or trying to determine the relationship, say, "I'd like to have a solid relationship with you. Do you want that, too?" This one's scary, especially if you're feeling like the relationship is on rocky ground. Asking the question is brave, as you're willing to broach the subject. It's so much better to know the answer than to wonder how they feel about you.

How to Overcome Someone's "No"

When someone says "no" to your business pitch, ask: "What concerns do you have?" or if you want to be even more polite, "May I ask what concerns you have?" You may be surprised at what this question could open up (more on this in Chapter 7).

How to Draw Someone Out

"Tell me more." This is by far the most powerful thing you can say to someone to make them feel heard and seen.

Plus, that will build better relationships and make you look amazing, too.

The challenge is remembering to pause after you say it and actually listen to what the other person has to say. Eye contact and leaning in (even on Zoom!) will show that you're present and ready to hear from them.

From an emotional intelligence perspective, saying this multiple times (even though it can feel strange) works, according to EQ expert Juliana Wilhelm. Reflective listening in between is particularly helpful. Such as, "What I'm hearing you say is...." followed by "tell me more" again. Then perhaps, "It sounds like..." and again, "tell me more."

Empathy is such an important skill, too. That will enable you to connect at an even deeper level and be seen as an influential leader. Everyone wants to know they're not alone.

STORYTELLING

People tend to think they have to be an amazing storyteller to tell stories. That's a myth.

THE TRUTH IS THAT STORIES CAN SIMPLY BE EXAMPLES.

Here are a few random prompts, particularly related to speaking about yourself. These can be great supplements to your introduction.

Storytelling Prompts

- The dream I've always had is...
- In 2018, something unexpected happened...
- Ever since I was a kid I...
- Most people thought I was nuts when...
- You won't believe what happened to me this weekend...

3 KEYS TO STORYTELLING

There are many different ways to tell stories, so consider these options for your toolbox. The most critical things to include are relevant details and emotion, along with a punchline. And keep it simple.

Here are some guidelines:

Structure:

Event X happened: Moved to SF

Caused X result: Found my calling

What you can learn/takeaway: Follow your heart and make your dream a reality

Example:

Event X happened: In 1994, I packed my bags, drove cross country from Minnesota to San Francisco, and never looked back.

Caused X result: After a career in corporate training and communications, working with clients such as Google, Facebook, and Netflix, I quickly found my love for speaking and my heart for encouraging women and realized they could mix. I had found my calling.

What you can learn/takeaway: It's possible to make your dreams a reality when you combine focus and action. Go for it!

Make it:

1. Relatable: can see themselves in it

2. Memorable: relevant details, emotion, help us picture it

3. Anticipatory: keep us guessing, curious

A FORMULA TO INTRODUCE YOURSELF

YOU WANT TO ALWAYS BE READY WITH YOUR INTRODUCTION. IT'S THE ONE THING WE HAVE THE LUXURY OF PREPARING IN ADVANCE.

Here's my PPU introduction formula

Personal: Say something personal (Minnesota, now San Francisco)

Professional: Share your profession (Professional speaker for high achieving corporate women over 40)

Unique: Offer something unique about you (I love following dreams—lived in Manhattan for my 50th birthday month)

Here's how it might sound in conversation:

I'm originally from Minnesota and now live in San Francisco, after packing my bags in the mid-90s to follow a dream of living in SF.

Professionally, I'm a speaker for high-achieving women who want to overcome self-doubt and speak with confidence instead. I specialize in executive presence and messaging and am on a mission to reach 10 million women.

Something unique about me is that I love adventure. An example of that is deciding to live in Manhattan for the month of October for my 50th birthday. I rented a place and spent 30 glorious days living like a local.

Try that out, and let me know how it goes! You'll sound prepared and focused, and leave your audience with something memorable about you.

Scan this QR Code for more details on how to introduce yourself."

YOUR ELEVATOR PITCH

Too often, elevator pitches sound scripted and unnatural. Take a lesson from Donald Miller (CEO of StoryBrand) and start with something relatable, getting them to nod in agreement. When you can bring forth a problem that's understandable and that they can empathize with, you're well on your way to getting your message through.

"WHAT I DO" PROMPTS

Option A: You know how (people and problem)? I help them to (solution). Thanks, Don.

Option B: I work with (people) who struggle with (pain), and I help them to instead (pleasure). Thanks, Jess Ekstrom.

Examples:

Option A: You know how women often hold back from sharing their ideas? I help them to overcome self-doubt and speak with confidence through their presence and their message so they can be seen as an influential leader.

Option B: I work with high achieving women who struggle with self-doubt, and I help them to speak with confidence through their presence and their message so they can be seen as an influential leader.

Option A: You know how many events have lackluster speakers? I'm on a mission to change that! I give corporate events a memorable experience by being an engaging speaker on leadership presence for women.

You may notice I'm biased toward Option A. It's most effective because of the relatability factor. The more you can use that in your communication, the more influential you will be.

9 WORDS TO AVOID AND WHAT TO SAY INSTEAD

There are many words we use by habit that take away from our credibility. Most of them we don't even realize! Full disclosure: some of these are phrases. Stick with me!

1. I'M SORRY

As women, we over apologize. "I'm sorry, could I interrupt?" "I'm sorry, could I ask you a question?" Train yourself to say "excuse me" instead. For example, you bump into someone at the grocery store. That would be a perfect time to say, "excuse me." There's no need to apologize. Only do that when you've legitimately wronged someone.

Let's say you're late for a meeting. Say "thank you for understanding" or "thanks for your patience." The other time you could use this is for a late response to an email. First of all, it's legit okay to respond within a day, but so many people think they have to apologize when it's taken them a few hours to respond. We have to rid ourselves of this habit! We don't have to be immediately available to people.

2. Does that make sense?

There's nothing like negating your own credibility when you ask if something made sense. When you ask this, it can look as if you weren't sure yourself if you made sense, and this takes away from your confidence. Instead, ask, "How did that land for you?" or "How was that helpful?" or "What questions do you have?" That way, you'll also get a more robust answer than what a closed-answered question would give you.

One other effect of saying this is that it can be perceived by the audience as if they're not capable of understanding, and that could come across as patronizing.

3. Ya' know what I mean?

Most likely, I don't [know what you mean]. Similar to "um" and "ah," this filler phrase is useless but has become so prevalent that we need to address it. It doesn't give information to contribute to a conversation; it's really a habit that acts as a way to make us as the speaker feel validated.

It can come across as if we're looking for agreement or buy-in, whether intentional or not. Instead, leave it out. If you really want to know if they know what you mean, ask a meaningful question such as "What was your biggest takeaway from that?" or "What resonates with you most about that?"

4. LITTLE AND JUST

Imagine if I said, "I just want to share a little tip with you." First off, "little" and "just" add no value to this sentence. "Little" is diminishing a valuable tip that you have, and "just" doubly acts as if it's dismissible and not that big of a deal. If you're going to bother to offer a tip, then drop the value-less words and say, "I want to share a tip with you." This comes across as much more confident and smart.

If you want to empower others who use the word "just," you can do what my friend Professor Gina Mertz, M.A., LMFT says, "There's nothing 'just' about what you just shared." What an encouraging and supportive way to increase self-awareness.

5. I THINK

This is often used as a habitual sentence starter and another filler phrase. Notice the difference between "I think this project would be a good investment" versus "This project would be a good investment." When we use "I think," it can sound like we're unsure, doubting ourselves, and lacking conviction. We diminish our credibility and impact. Yet, it's used so much that it's practically automatic. It's often paired with a tentative and/or soft vocal tone, making it even less effective.

Side note: Saying "I think X" when you want to share your opinion is different (and A-okay!). If you've heard me talk about this before, I'm a big advocate of saying, "Here's my vote" or "Here's what I think." It's all about the intent behind your words.

6. For me AND I want you to

Have you ever been to the gym and the trainer says something to the tune of: "Do another ten reps for me!" or "Pedal harder for me!"? Why would I want to do this for the trainer? Your audience should be motivated to do something because there's a BENEFIT to them, not because you (as the speaker) want them to do it. Now, the audience may like and respect you, but the point is that you and your message will be more relevant to them when you leave "for me" out of the equation. In addition, you'll be more direct. Notice how the meaning only becomes stronger when you say, "Do another ten reps!"

"I want you to" is in the same category. How often do you hear, "I want you to work on this project," or "I want you to write this down." If you eliminate "I want you to," you'll be more concise, direct, and audience-focused. True inspiration and transformation come from someone wanting to do it because they're internally motivated. Instead, say: "Write this down." This might sound too direct, but with the appropriate tone and facial expression, it will be quite effective.

"I need you to" is similar. We sound desperate when we say this. It can bring up a power dynamic along with the earlier logic about positioning a message to our audience's needs, not based on what we want or need. A true leader invites people to do things because they make it irresistible, not because of fear or power.

7. Kinda, sorta, maybe

These words are in the same camp because they're all modifiers and value-diminishers. They make us sound unsure and tentative; the opposite of confidence. Think of an economy of words. If every word cost us $20, we'd think about each one with much more intention. You want to be concise and share value in each word. Taking these out will help you do that.

For example, say, "This would be a value to our company because of XYZ," instead of, "I kinda sorta maybe think this would be a benefit to our company." Or, on a personal note, imagine hearing your partner say, "I kinda love you." What??!!

8. But

We've all heard of the effectiveness of the "Yes, and" concept from improv...because it works! Moving an idea forward using "and" instead of "but" is much more collaborative and inviting. As soon as we hear the word "but" it negates everything that was said before it. It's a small word with a tremendous amount of negative power. See if you can eliminate this word from your vocabulary.

Hot tip: sometimes replacing "but" with "and" doesn't always work, but putting a period at the end of the sentence and then starting a new sentence works fabulously. For example, "I know we had talked about a salary increase last year. While we don't have the budget for that, what we will do is..." instead of "I know we had talked about a salary increase last year, but we don't have the budget for it." UGH. Who wants to hear that? As human beings, we want options. We want to know what we CAN do. Focus on that as you move your ideas forward.

9. I HOPE

While doing a mock interview with a client recently, I was reminded of this one. She kept saying things like "I hope to bring the department to a new level" or "I hope that my skills and experience will translate well." To that I say, "Stop!" Instead, use "I plan" or anything else, really! For example. "I plan to bring the department to a new level" or "My plan is to use my skills and experience in this new role." You could also use "My goal is..." or "I'm excited to..."

Using "hope" in this context makes us sound doubtful and uncertain. When we're interviewing for a new job or to secure a new client, we need to sound 100% sure of our abilities and what we can offer.

RECAP:

To *sorta* recap, *I'm sorry* that this was so long, *but I hope it made sense. I think I maybe just* wanted to share a few *little* tips with you. *Ya' know what I mean? I want you to* use these strategies *for me, but I kinda want you to* use them for you.

Now...to recap for *real*. This all rolls up to one main idea: Speak with intention if you want to influence and make a meaningful impact.

If you'd like this in PDF format scan here:

CONCLUSION

TIME TO CELEBRATE

Congratulations! You have everything you need to succeed. Let's celebrate.

You can trust your own voice, empower yourself, and step into your confidence.

Remember that transformation happens in stages, so be kind to yourself through this process. It will get easier and easier as you take each step.

It's high time for you to speak up, stand out, and be the unstoppable force you were meant to be.

The world is waiting for you.

ACKNOWLEDGMENTS

Chris Laos, thank you for being the greatest fan of my life. I love you.

Mom, your strength of character and kindness of heart transcend time.

Dad, thank you for showing me the value of persistence and determination.

Townsend Leadership friends, you are forever part of the sacred space where I grew most.

Don Miller and Ally Fallon, thank you for creating the structure and the space for me to write my story.

Ann Kroeker, thank you for challenging me to make Chapter 1 the very best version possible.

Hollis Citron, your encouragement to write this book myself, and in whatever way I wanted, was a breath of fresh air.

Amber Glus, you've elevated my business in ways I couldn't have imagined, including the entire process of this book operation. Dani Hamlet, thank you for your tireless work and problem solving abilities (you remain, as advertised!). Lauren Hanley, thank you for saying "yes" to doing my book cover!

Carly Mask and Sarah Bailey of Camp Digital, you brought the design of my brand vision to life back in 2020. To say you exceeded expectations is an understatement.

Larry Habegger, thank you for your expertise and brotherly guidance.

Thank you to the countless friends and family members who have supported me along the way.

NOTE FROM THE AUTHOR

EPILOGUE

I never expected it to turn out this way. Not in my wildest dreams. God knew all along that I would be writing this book myself, and I'm so glad I did. But I didn't exactly choose that, at first.

In October of 2021 I heard a ghostwriter on Clubhouse and became mezmerized that I could have a published book by Spring of 2022 without having to write it myself. I'd always wondered why people hire ghostwriters; if I'm honest, I always thought that was a way out of doing it yourself. If I wanted to write a book, why would I hire someone else to write it for me?

Turns out hiring a ghostwriter felt like the best choice for me given the busyness of my schedule and not having to do the work. Wow, was I wrong in that last part!

He was a disaster. After months of waiting I got the first draft and it was terrible. Within 24 hours I knew I had to write the book myself. But I hadn't faced that yet.

Driving to the gym the morning after getting the draft, I thought, "He didn't even get the point of my book!" Then I had to turn the tables on myself and ask, "What *is* the point of your book?" Yikes. Maybe I wasn't clear enough. Maybe I never said it. Then it hit me: "It's to trust your *own* voice!" I had another realization: "I'm not famous yet! No one cares about my story. They care about themselves. They need practical tips. Not just a few sprinkled throughout my story, but a whole host of them. That needs to *be* the story."

As I started on the 22T treadmill that morning, I thought, "I have to write this book myself." And after my workout, I parked at the Marina Green in San Francisco with the Golden Gate Bridge to my left and started writing the outline of the book you have in your hands..

In 45 minutes, I wrote out the ten Chapters and subpoints. It flowed out of me. It was a divine download. Thank You, Jesus.

It took awhile for me to face that I truly did have to write this myself, but once I did, I started writing every day. That was the beginning of April, 2022. My deadline was April 30. If I wanted to have this book done in time for a June publish date, then I had to do it quickly.

In three weeks, I wrote this book. Well, the bulk of it. It first started at the Write Your Story workshop with Donald Miller and Ally Fallon. That's where I learned a powerful story structure. There, the first chapter was born. It's also the chapter that took the most heart. I hired a phenomenal writing coach (Ann Kroeker). I wrote all over the city of San Francisco, mostly from the passenger seat of my car.

Never did I imagine I would do it this way, but it became magical. It was the hardest thing I've done in a long time and it was well worth it. I learned the power of focus in a way that I couldn't have experienced without doing this. Head down every day, you can make things happen; often quicker than you expect.

You may have a book in you, too. Start writing. Get to know yourself through the process. You'll find new insights about yourself that you didn't see before. That's the power of writing your story.

KAREN LAOS BIO

Karen Laos is a former corporate leader turned professional speaker specializing in communication. She is fiercely committed to equipping women in business to speak with clarity and stand out with unshakable confidence.

Over her 20+ year career, she has gained rave reviews from clients such as NASA, Facebook, Google, Netflix, Sephora, AT&T, Levi's and United Healthcare.

If you're looking for a speaker to make your event memorable, she's available and can be reached at hello@karenlaos.com.

Karen got her start in human resources at Gap Inc and then found her passion for corporate training at Decker Communications, where she led a team of facilitators and traveled the globe consulting professionals on their communication skills. After 14 years, she left Decker in 2020 to pursue her entrepreneurial dream (and hasn't looked back!).

Her mission is to eradicate self-doubt so women can stop holding back and start taking their seat at the table. One of the ways she does this is through her podcast: Ignite Your

Confidence with Karen Laos. Her plan is to reach 10 million women in the next ten years.

Karen's style is approachable and engaging. She connects quickly and leaves audiences feeling empowered with practical tools they can apply immediately.

She lives in San Francisco with her husband who is the love of her life (Chris Laos), along with their two kitties, Mojo and Callie.

Fun fact: To follow her dream of living in Manhattan, she rented an apartment for a month to celebrate her 50th birthday.